Responding to Self-Harm in
Children and Adolescents

by the same author

The Social Worker's Guide to Child and Adolescent Mental Health
Steven Walker
Foreword by Stephen Briggs
ISBN 978 1 84905 122 4

of related interest

By Their Own Young Hand
Deliberate Self-harm and Suicidal Ideas in Adolescents
Keith Hawton and Karen Rodham
With Emma Evans
ISBN 978 1 84310 230 4

Deliberate Self-Harm in Adolescence
Claudine Fox and Keith Hawton
ISBN 978 1 84310 237 3
Child and Adolescent Mental Health series

Cutting it Out
A Journey through Psychotherapy and Self-Harm
Carolyn Smith
Foreword by Maggie Turp
ISBN 978 1 84310 266 3

Working with Suicidal Individuals
A Guide to Providing Understanding, Assessment and Support
Tony White
ISBN 978 1 84905 115 6

Supporting Traumatized Children and Teenagers
A Guide to Providing Understanding and Help
Atle Dyregrov
ISBN 978 1 84905 034 0

Cognitive Behavioural Therapy for Child Trauma and Abuse
A Step-by-Step Approach
Jacqueline S. Feather and Kevin R. Ronan
ISBN 978 1 84905 086 9

Children and Adolescents in Trauma
Creative Therapeutic Approaches
Edited by Chris Nicholson, Michael Irwin and Kedar N Dwivedi
Foreword by Peter Wilson
ISBN 978 1 84310 437 7
Community, Culture and Change series

Responding to Self-Harm in Children and Adolescents

A Professional's Guide to Identification, Intervention and Support

Steven Walker

Jessica Kingsley *Publishers*
London and Philadelphia

First published in 2012
by Jessica Kingsley Publishers
116 Pentonville Road
London N1 9JB, UK
and
400 Market Street, Suite 400
Philadelphia, PA 19106, USA

www.jkp.com

Library of Congress Cataloging in Publication Data
A CIP catalog record for this book is available from the Library of Congress

British Library Cataloguing in Publication Data
A CIP catalogue record for this book is available from the British Library

ISBN 978 1 84905 172 9
eISBN 978 0 85700 306 5

Printed and bound in Great Britain

Acknowledgements

My deepest and heartfelt thanks to all those children and young people, parents, carers, colleagues and students I have known and worked with over the past 30 years from whom I have gained considerable inspiration, knowledge and learning. In particular I am indebted to the huge numbers of writers, researchers, academics and professional staff whose work has influenced and supported my investigation into self-harm and suicide. The work of self-help organisations, charities and young people trying to help themselves has greatly assisted my research and enriched this text. Where possible I have included references to source material/websites and published papers but any omissions are my responsibility and will be corrected if any are missing and drawn to my attention. I am especially grateful to Jessica Kingsley Publishers especially Stephen Jones and Carolyn Holleyman for their support, patience and professionalism.

Contents

Introduction

The World Health Organization has predicted that mental illness is set to become the biggest public health challenge of the 21st century (WHO 2009). The latest government mental health strategy document (see Appendix 1) referring to the treatment and support for young people who self-harm (DoH 2011) acknowledges the seriousness of the problem in the UK. While not every young person who self-harms has a mental illness nevertheless, it is a risk factor.

Latest research from the UK Government (House of Commons 2011) reveals some stark statistics:

- Over the last ten years inpatient admissions for young people have increased by 68 per cent due to self-harm.

- Last year alone hospital inpatient admissions for under 25s increased by 10 per cent due to self-harm.

- Amongst females under 25 there has been a 77 per cent increase in the last ten years in inpatient admissions due to self-harm.

This book aims to provide a resource for professionals such as nurses, social workers, youth workers, and teachers in a variety of contexts in voluntary or statutory agencies who may encounter situations where concerns are expressed about the behaviour, emotional state, or mental health of a child or young person. This could be in child protection, young offenders, hospital and primary health, family support, long-term planning, fostering and adoption, juvenile justice, education, social care, probation, and of course child and adolescent mental health services.

Staff who initially come into contact with a young person who has self-harmed are crucial not just in terms of immediate physical aid but in setting the scene for how well the young person copes and moves on (NICE 2004). Unfortunately staff attitudes are generally poor, making the young person feel worse and compromising any opportunity for future support and help (see Appendix 2). The book aspires to provide a foundation of theoretical ideas and practical guidance that will offer support and create the basis for informed, reflective, confident practice. I'm primarily addressing a professional audience concerned about this serious problem, though in some circumstances professionals may choose to pass on a copy to carers, parents or even young people themselves.

If a young person causes physical harm to their body in order to deal with overwhelming feelings, they have nothing to be ashamed of. It's important as a professional to acknowledge that this is their way of keeping themselves alive and maintaining psychological integrity with the only tool they have right now. It's a crude and ultimately self-destructive tool, but it works; they get relief from the overwhelming pain/fear/anxiety in their life. The prospect of giving it up may be unthinkable, which makes sense; because they may not realise that self-harm isn't the only or even best coping method around.

For many people who self-harm, though, there comes a moment when they realise that change is possible, that they can escape, that things can be different. They begin to believe that other tools *do* exist and begin figuring out which of these non self-destructive ways of coping work for them. How do you know if someone you know self-harms? It may seem an odd question to some, but a few people aren't sure if what they do is 'really' self-injury. At the right time try asking these questions or at least think about them yourself as the professional concerned:

1. Do they deliberately cause physical harm to themselves to the extent of causing tissue damage (breaking the skin, bruising, leaving marks that last for more than an hour)?

2. Do they cause this harm to themselves as a way of dealing with unpleasant or overwhelming emotions, thoughts, or situations (including dissociation)?

3. If the self-harm is not compulsive, do they often think about self-harm even when they are relatively calm and not doing it at the moment?

If they answer yes to 1 and 2, they are a self-harmer. If they answer yes to 3, they are most likely a repetitive self-harmer. The way they choose to hurt themselves could be cutting, hitting, burning, scratching, skin-picking, banging their head, breaking bones, not letting wounds heal, among others. They might do several of these. How they injure themselves isn't as important as recognising that they do and what it means in their life.

Self-harming behaviour does not necessarily mean they were an abused child. That said, there are young people who self-harm who have a nasty history of emotional, physical and sexual abuse. So you don't have to start jumping to conclusions or triggering unnecessary strong, disruptive interventions. It can indicate that somewhere along the line, they didn't learn good ways of coping with overwhelming feelings. Keep all your options open in terms of developing hypotheses and assessment processes.

Professionals need to work very hard to assure the young person they are not a disgusting person or sick; rather they should try to suggest that they just never learned positive ways to deal with their feelings.

Note on the Appendices: Appendix 1 sets the overall context for government policy and will be useful for those requiring knowledge of up-to-date government guidance. Appendix 2 is crucial in containing knowledge about staff attitudes and service users' experiences, with some direct quotes. This information is critical in the management and care of self-harming young people, and readers will appreciate having access to respected data from NICE guidelines. Appendix 3 is a list of useful resources and organisations, including several self-harm websites and helplines. The list is derived from multiple sources all focused on children and young people – all of whom (especially disabled children), are susceptible to self-harm. Reference to them has been made in the chapters, explaining their relevance to the readership.

Recommended further reading

Alderman, T. *The Scarred Soul: Understanding and Ending Self-inflicted Violence*. Oakland, CA: New Harbinger Publications.

Arnold, L. and Magill, A. *The Self-harm Help Book*. Abergavenny: The Basement Project.

Pembroke, L. R. *Self-harm: Perspectives from Personal Experience*. London: Chipmunkapublishing.

Strong, M. *A Bright Red Scream: Self-Mutilation and the Language of Pain*. New York, USA: Penguin.

Sutton, J. *Healing the Hurt Within: Understand Self-injury and Self-harm, and Heal the Emotional Wounds*. Oxford: How To Books Ltd.

CHAPTER 1

Understanding Self-Harm

What is self-harm?

Deliberate self-harm has been defined as 'causing deliberate hurt to your own body, most commonly by cutting, but also by burning, abusing drugs, alcohol or other substances.' Another description is to call the problem self injury 'as a way of dealing with difficult feelings, by cutting, burning or bruising, taking an overdose of tablets, pulling hair or picking skin.' Young people at risk of developing this problem are usually 14+ year-old adolescents who are depressed, have low self-esteem or have been sexually abused (www.thesite. org/healthandwellbeing/mentalhealth/selfharm).

The definition of self-harm is also associated with 'attempted suicide', 'parasuicide', 'suicidal gestures' and 'manipulative attempts'. These terms are widely used by a variety of health and welfare professionals and can lead to confusion for parents and those trying to help the troubled young person. Most young people with this problem are not actually attempting suicide in that they do not start off with a plan to end their own life.

The World Health Organization defines parasuicide as:

> an act with a non-fatal outcome, in which an individual deliberately initiates a non-habitual behaviour, that without intervention from others, will cause self-harm or deliberately ingests a substance in excess of the prescribed or generally recognised therapeutic

dosage, and which is aimed at realising changes which the subject desired via the actual or expected physical consequences. (WHO 2011, p.112)

However, it is important when trying to understand this problem to distinguish between young people who want to die, those who do not want to die and those who are ambivalent as to whether they die or not, in order to design the most effective way to help. Self-harm may help someone to cope with feelings that threaten to overwhelm them; painful emotions, such as rage, sadness, emptiness, grief, self-hatred, fear, loneliness and guilt. These can be released through the body, where they can be seen and dealt with.

Self-harm may serve a number of purposes at the same time. It may be a way of getting the pain out, of being distracted from it, of communicating feelings to somebody else, and of finding comfort. It can also be a means of self-punishment or an attempt to gain some control over life. Because they may feel ashamed, afraid, or worried about other people's reactions, people who self-harm often conceal what they are doing rather than draw attention to it.

It's worth remembering that most people behave self-destructively at times, even if they don't realise it. Perfectly ordinary behaviour, such as smoking, eating and drinking too much, or working long hours, day after day, can all be helping people to numb or distract themselves and avoid being alone with their thoughts and feelings.

How common is this problem?

Research in this area has only been conducted in recent years as the problem has come to the attention of more and more parents, teachers, social workers and all staff who are in regular contact with children and young people.

Mental health problems in general among young people have been rising in developed countries over the past 25 years

(Walker 2010). One American study discovered that thoughts of suicide are not uncommon among teenagers particularly those experimenting with drugs and other substances:

> 27 per cent of 14 to 17-year-olds thought about suicide in the previous 12-month period.
>
> 16 per cent made a specific plan.
>
> 8 per cent made an attempt.
>
> 2 per cent received medical attention.
>
> (Rowan 2001, p.86)

In England and Wales there are about 25,000 admissions to accident and emergency hospital departments for deliberate self-harm each year. However, the way data on suicide and self-harm are collated is problematic. This is because there is inconsistency in data collection from coroners and hospital records using different definitions and more importantly, because most self-harming behaviour does not come to the attention of the emergency services or health and welfare staff. Shame and stigma deter many from seeking help.

Since many acts of self-harm do not come to the attention of healthcare services, hospital attendance rates do not reflect the true scale of the problem (Hawton *et al.* 2002; Meltzer *et al.* 2000). A national interview survey suggested that in Great Britain between 4.6 per cent and 6.6 per cent of people have self-harmed (Meltzer *et al.* 2000). However, even this might be an under-estimate. In a school survey, 13 per cent of young people aged 15 or 16 reported having self-harmed at some time in their lives and 7 per cent as having done so in the previous year.

In the USA self-harm appears to be more prevalent than in Europe or Canada. In the USA anonymous surveys of high school students revealed rates of 8.5 per cent compared with rates of 3.5 per cent in Canada, and 2.2 per cent in Europe (Laye-Gindhu and Schonert-Reichl 2005). The number of emergency department visits for self-inflicted injury in the USA in 2007 was 472,000. In Australia the number of self-harming behaviours in young people has increased over recent years. In 2005–2006, there were 7299 hospitalisations of young people due to intentional self-harm – a rate of 197 per 100,000 young people (Harrison, Moller and Bordeaux 2011).

Many parents who are shocked and frightened will try to help their child themselves or seek private help from counsellors/therapists. How each family reacts to and deals with the problem will have some bearing on how quickly the young person recovers and comes to terms with their actions. This means that matters can worsen, stay the same, or resolve quite quickly. For example, interrogating the young person or criticising will only lower further their self-esteem, discussing how they feel and what can be changed to help them stop is better. As a professional you need to be sensitive to how parents/carers express their distress so that your communication needs to be carefully worded to avoid leaving the young person with burdensome guilt feelings.

Much will depend on the resilience and coping culture within the family. For example, how have previous individual problems been managed? Have they been hidden and 'swept under the carpet'? Are emotions easily expressed or bottled up prior to exploding? Is the family 'enmeshed' – so close and tight that there is too little time and space for individuals to exercise some free expression? Or is the family so fluid that they act as separate individuals, hardly communicating, eating separately, watching TV on their own?

There is no correct way for families to operate, but it is important that they, together with professional help, can understand how they function, communicate and interact in order to establish a baseline of where they are at. Awareness of this (which might come as a surprise to some family members) provides the context for change if that is desirable or even possible. Crucial to any success is to cancel any blaming, finger pointing, or digging up old conflicts and accusations – this will only make matters worse and harder to gain success.

Who is likely to self-harm?

According to research, the majority are young women, although the percentage of young men seems to be on the increase. Self-harming behaviour is also significant among minority groups discriminated against by society. Someone who has mental health problems is more likely to self-harm. So are those who are dependent on drugs or alcohol, or who are faced with a number of major life problems, such as being homeless, a single parent, in financial difficulty or otherwise living in stressful circumstances.

A common factor is often a feeling of helplessness or powerlessness with regard to their emotions. Self-harm involves all of us on some level. We may all punish, distract or numb ourselves as a way of dealing with difficult feelings or situations (Briggs 2002).

Recent research (Mental Health Foundation 2006) focusing on young people suggests that 10 per cent of 15 to 16-year-olds have self-harmed, usually by cutting themselves, and that girls are far more likely to self-harm than boys. The most common reason is 'to find relief from a terrible situation'. Young people are often under great pressure within their families, from school and among their peers. Many young people report having friends who they know also self-harm.

The research suggests that young people who self-harm are much more likely to have low self-esteem, to be depressed and anxious. They seem to be facing more problems in life, but may be less good at coping with them. They may retreat into themselves, feeling angry, blaming themselves, tending to drink and smoke too much and to use more recreational drugs (ONS 2008). They confide in fewer friends, and tend not to talk to their parents or other adults, or to ask for the help they need.

- About 1 in 10 young people will self-harm at some point, but it can occur at any age.

- It is more common in young women than men.

- Self-harm is more common in some groups of people, such as prisoners, asylum seekers and veterans of the armed forces.

- Gay, lesbian and bisexual people are more likely to self-harm than heterosexual people. Researchers think that this is may be due at least in part to the stress individuals may experience as a result of prejudice and discrimination.

- Sometimes groups of young people self-harm together. Having a friend who self-harms may increase the chances of doing it as well.

- People who self-harm are more likely to have experienced physical, emotional or sexual abuse during childhood. (p.108)

Socially excluded children and their families

Black children

Despite the years of rhetoric of anti-racist and anti-oppressive practice, professional assessments and care planning are still generally inadequate. Assessments are often partial and rarely cover parental capacity, the child's needs, and environmental issues. There is little evidence that care planning takes a lifelong view – highlighting the failure to recruit black foster carers or understanding the changing characteristics of this group of children. The mental health needs of black children who self-harm are virtually ignored. Guidance (DoH/DCSF 2005) suggests:

- ensuring that services and staffing are monitored by ethnicity to ensure they are provided appropriately and equally

- involving ethnic minorities in planning and reviewing services

- training in anti-racist and anti-discriminatory practice

- investigating and monitoring complaints of racial discrimination or harassment

- explicit policies are in place for working with black families.

Continual reflection and evaluation of practice is required to maintain an anti-racist socially inclusive practice. Recognising racial harassment as a child protection issue and as an indicator for subsequent potential mental health problems such as self-harm is evidence of the translation of policy generalisation into specific practice change.

Workers who make sure they take full account of a child's religion, racial, cultural and linguistic background in the decision making process are demonstrating the link between social policy and socially inclusive practice. Ensuring that black children in residential care have access to advocates and positive role models can assist in challenging institutionally racist practice.

A socially inclusive practice will help develop strategies to overcome value judgements about the superiority of white family culture and norms. Exploring the impact of white power and privileges in relationships with black people and drawing connections between racism and the social control elements of public health practice, is another example. Rejecting stereotypes of black and ethnic minority family structures and relationships will enable staff to assess the rich cultural, linguistic and spiritual diversity of family life and permit the building of an assessment not based on a deficit model judged against an anglocentric norm (Fernando 2002).

There is strong evidence that the experience of racism affects the mental health prospects of black children; therefore efforts to protect black children from racism and racist abuse is a priority within a socially inclusive practice (Lemos and Crane 2011). Recent research (O'Brian, Moules and Walker 2010, p.48) revealed:

- Racism and racial bullying are commonplace within the lives of ethnic minority children and young people.

- The most common expression of racism is through racist name-calling previously considered by adults as trivial but the impact is now known to be profound.

- Racial bullying frequently involves the use of violence.

- Violence against ethnic minority groups is persistent, patterned, and long-term in the way it affects individuals and the places where they live.

Disabled children

Disabled children and those with learning difficulties are more likely to have mental health problems than other children. Disabled children and adolescents are twice as likely to have emotional and behavioural problems which can lead to self-harm/mutilation.

There are a growing number of disabled children and young people living in the community who need high levels of support. Partly this is because more of these children are surviving infancy, and partly because there is no longer the assumption that disabled children should be cared for in hospitals or other institutions (Walker 2010).

Lone parents with disabled children, families from ethnic minorities, and families caring for the most severely disabled children have the highest levels of unmet need, and live in the poorest conditions. The mental health needs of disabled children are often masked by a narrow focus on their disability through a medical, rather than social model of disability.

Behaviour causing concern such as head-banging, scratching or other forms of self-harm can often be ascribed to the physical or intellectual disability rather than a separate psychological need.

Disabled children with a severe disability need to know how to deal with the social and psychological challenges they face – including dealing with other family members, coping with their own negative feelings, and planning for the future. Families require relief and request a range of support including home-based sitting services, residential or family-based respite care, or long-term care from social services departments. Needs change over time.

For instance, a family with an autistic child may want a graded range of services. In the early years they want information and support with their child's development. When the child is a bit older they need respite care. But when the children reach early teens the research says about 60 per cent of families want their child to be accommodated by public services (Sicile-Kira 2003).

Disability discrimination legislation in several countries expects that social services and health service providers must not discriminate against disabled children by refusing to provide any service which is provided to other children, by providing a lower standard of service or offering a service on less favourable terms. Service providers will have to take reasonable measures to remove, alter, or provide reasonable means of avoiding physical features that make it impossible or unreasonably difficult for disabled children to use the services including when they are undertaking or contributing to assessments.

This means access to child and adolescent mental health services needs to be considered from the disabled child's perspective. A socially inclusive practice would link with local disabled children's networks and involve parent/carers and children in the planning and delivery of necessary changes particularly increasing awareness of self-harm and suicide risk (Oldman and Beresford 1998).

The mental health needs of deaf children like other disabled children are often overlooked or simply poorly understood. The medical model of disability ensures that the disability itself is the focus of attention rather than the disabling environment and attitudes of society which can lower self-esteem and provoke self-harm.

Very little research has been undertaken with this particularly socially excluded group to try to understand their emotional and psychological needs and the impact on them of their disability. Deaf culture needs to be taken into account if a socially inclusive practice is to be employed by workers. Its principle characteristics are:

- sharing a common language (BSL) for communication purposes

- social interaction choices

- identity issues

- historic understanding of discrimination.

Deaf BSL users view their deafness as a cultural identity, they are proud of their language and feel they belong to a linguistic minority group. They do not want their deafness to be cured and are more concerned about improved access to services, information and democracy. Various disability rights organisations have been established to act as a watchdog for implementation of disability discrimination legislation.

The low uptake of respite services by Asian parents with a disabled child are still perceived by some as evidence of the closed network of familial relationships within Asian culture, rather than evidence of the inaccessibility of existing service provision.

Sometimes this is a matter of proper translating services being unavailable, but it can also represent a lack of effort from social workers and other healthcare professionals to properly understand the families they aspire to help. For example, some Asian families are reluctant to have daughters cared for by male carers, or they simply have little knowledge of the health and welfare systems.

Self-harm is likely to be even more of a taboo subject in some cultures where facial markings are part of ancient ritualistic norms and female genital mutilation is widely practised (Walker 2005). Even when good translators are available they do not always manage to convey the subtleties of meaning related to feelings and cultural differences.

Young offenders

In 2000, one out of three young black men was either locked up, on probation, or on parole in the USA, while recent data reveal that in total there were 7800 juveniles imprisoned (Home Office 2008). According to recent figures there were 11,500 young people aged 15 to 20 in jail in England and Wales; of those 90 per cent had a diagnosable mental health disorder, which had been missed in their initial medical assessment, many had substance abuse problems as well as personality disorders. Sixty per cent had anxiety and depressive illness, with 10 per cent suffering from a severe psychotic mental illness such as schizophrenia.

Twenty per cent of these young men and 40 per cent of young women will have attempted suicide prior to their imprisonment with many having a history of self-harm. In Australia over 5000 young people are estimated to be imprisoned, with disproportionate numbers of aboriginal youth in the prison population (AIHW 2001). Young offenders are among the most socially excluded groups in society and the evidence suggests that imprisonment simply makes matters worse, not better. Within two years of release, 75 per cent will have been reconvicted and 47 per cent will be back in jail (Social Exclusion Unit 2002). If some of these young people become homeless or end up in insecure accommodation, they are between 8 and 11 times more likely to develop mental health problems leading to self-harm or suicide.

Low take-up of preventive mental health services among socially excluded families means that minor problems can develop into major problems. Over 90 per cent of recidivist juvenile delinquents had a conduct disorder as children. The estimated annual cost per child if conduct disorder is left untreated is £15,270. Forty per cent of 7 to 8-year-olds with an untreated conduct disorder became recidivist delinquents as teenagers. Young offenders are three times as likely to have a mental health problem as other young people. Yet these problems are often neglected because there are no proper methods for screening and assessing mental health problems within youth justice systems (Mental Health Foundation 2002).

The evidence shows that more than 25 per cent of young men and 41 per cent of young women under 21 in prison had received treatment for mental health problems in the year before they were jailed and young people were statistically more likely to be the victims rather than the perpetrators of crime.

Once in the prison system, a lack of purposeful activity, long hours in cells, and a climate of brutality and bullying can reinforce negative attitudes and magnify underlying mental health problems. Prison is no place for young people with mental health problems. The risk of self-harm and suicide is all too evident, with frequent reports of these practices in young offenders' institutions.

Even the most progressive regimes are inadequate to the task of meeting these already damaged individuals' needs. They require stability, certainty, care, and proper support to tackle their offending behaviour within a context of restorative justice and personal responsibility, backed up by nurturing, therapeutic input (MacNeil, Dressler and Kaufman 2000).

Children in public care

Nearly 60,000 children were being looked after by public authorities in the UK in 2011. About 60 per cent of these children had been abused or neglected with a further 10 per cent coming from 'dysfunctional families' (Home Office 2008). Abuse of this nature can lead to self-harming behaviour, severe behavioural problems and depression.

Evidence confirms that the mental health needs of these children and young people are overlooked and that many have established mental health problems prior to coming into local authority care. A total of 38,400 of these children were in foster placements and 6400 were in children's homes, yet foster carers and residential staff are among the least qualified and supported people left to manage sometimes extreme behaviour (DoH 2007).

Specialist mental health services often decline to help because of the uncertain and possibly temporary nature of the child's placement which contra-indicates successful intervention. The dilemma is that without input, placements often break down as carers cannot cope, invariably leading to more placements and further deterioration in the child's mental health (Richardson and Joughin 2000).

Recent research emphasises the importance of a preventive approach with children in the public care system who are more likely to be excluded from school following emotional and behavioural difficulties. Teacher training that fails to adequately prepare newly qualified staff to respond to the mental health needs of pupils is considered to be a factor in the increased use of school exclusions (DfES 2006).

Social workers and other professionals such as school nurses using a preventive approach could be helpful to teaching staff and organise collaborative work aimed at preventing difficult behaviour escalating. Unless the mental health needs of these children and young people are addressed as part of a strategy that effectively nurtures children's inclusion in school the risk of deterioration is high. The risk factors for looked after children are probably the most extreme of any socially excluded group and could trigger self-harming behaviour. They include:

- developmental delay
- school failure
- communication difficulty
- low self-esteem
- parent/carer conflict
- family breakdown
- rejection
- abuse
- parental mental illness
- alcohol/drug abuse
- poverty
- homelessness
- loss.

Children with HIV/AIDS

The stress experienced by children and families infected with HIV is magnified by societal attitudes and prejudice about HIV/AIDS, and is a risk factor for the development of mental health problems in children and adolescents. These are some of the psycho-social stressors that can contribute towards the social exclusion of these vulnerable families:

- *Stigma and fear of contagion* – this can produce alienation and rejection by peers of children with HIV/AIDS. Parents can lose employment or become homeless as a result of perceived risks.

- *Shame, guilt and anger* – the stigma can produce intense feelings of shame, guilt and anger which are difficult to manage within the family system. Professionals may also blame drug abusing parents for causing their child's illness further reinforcing feelings of despair.

- *Secrecy and social isolation* – families often live in secrecy with their diagnosis and the associated stigma of homosexuality, drug abuse or prostitution. The consequent social isolation and rejection from extended family support systems can trigger depression, suicidal thoughts, and poor compliance with medical care.

Denial and fleeing medical facilities are not uncommon responses to a positive diagnosis particularly among adults with alcohol or other substance abuse habits. The emotional shock following a period of denial may be characterised by intense feelings of hysteria and anger followed by depressive symptoms, withdrawal and feelings of shame and guilt.

Unless these feelings are managed and contained in a helping relationship they will affect the emotional temperature in the household and pose a further risk to the mental health of children in the family (Pollock and Boland 1990). The potential for self-harm is magnified in these circumstances, therefore workers need to bear in mind that a simple referral about a child with emerging mental health problems could involve a child in the centre of an emotional whirlwind where the underlying cause cannot be revealed.

Working with HIV infected children requires similar skills to working with any child or adolescent with added emphasis on issues of trust, time, loss, secrecy and bereavement. Understanding the child's conception of the illness is a crucial task. This can build on what the child or young person already understands about chronic illness causality in general.

The key is in adapting knowledge and information to the developmental level the child is at in order for effective communication to take place. An important and difficult issue is the decision about whether and when to disclose the diagnosis to the child. Conflicts between family members and professionals can take place over this most sensitive issue, and affect the emotional state of the child. These principles are generally followed:

- The truth is generally less threatening to a child than fear of the unknown.

- Information needs to be presented at a level that is developmentally appropriate for the child.

- Disclosure is a *process* not an *event*.

Refugee and asylum-seeking children

The number of applications for asylum from unaccompanied under 18s almost trebled in recent years in the UK. Data indicates that there were more than 6000 unaccompanied asylum-seeking children supported by local authorities (Refugee Action 2006).

Further evidence shows that many of these young people were accommodated and receiving a worse service than other children in need (Elliot 2007). Very little research has been done to ascertain the mental health needs of this group of children. However, there is some evidence of the symptoms of post-traumatic stress syndrome being present before they then experience the racist xenophobic abuse of individuals and institutions incapable of demonstrating humanitarian concern for their plight.

This combination can shatter the most psychologically robust personality. It has been estimated that serious mental health disorders may be present in 40–50 per cent of young refugees with increased likelihood of self-harm a direct consequence (Hodes 2000).

The evidence for the need to distinguish the different mental health needs of all children in a culturally diverse society and protect them from racist abuse is strong. For example, refugee and asylum-seeking children, some unaccompanied, many affected by extreme circumstances, might include those witnessing murder of parents or kin (Walker 2005). They will also have experienced dislocation from school and community, severing of important friendships and extended family support, loss of home, and prolonged insecurity.

These experiences will likely trigger symptoms consistent with post-traumatic stress syndrome. This is manifested in a variety of ways including self-harming behaviour. Each individual child or adolescent will react differently according to variables such as:

- the context of their departure from the home country

- the family cohesion and coping capacity

- the child's own personality and predisposing psychological constitution

- proximity to extreme acts of murder or violence

- the child's developmental stage and history of transition.

A number of studies compared levels of stress in adolescents and family functioning across different national boundaries including Canada, USA, Britain, Malaysia, India, Hong Kong and the Philippines. A meta-analysis of these studies tested the hypothesis that while subjectively perceived levels of stress can vary significantly between cultures, the underlying causes of personal distress could be relatively similar between cultures (Van Ijzendoorn and Sagi 1997). This is useful information to consider when trying to practise in culturally competent ways, which avoid racist stereotyping (Walker and Thurston 2006).

The differences in reported prevalence rates of mental health problems in various countries may reflect different classification systems, rather than real differences. Therefore, family dysfunction as perceived by the child or adolescent will, with other perceived stressors, be a statistically significant predictor of self-harm and emotional states in all ethnic groups.

The conclusion is that there is a measurable, culturally universal, aspect of the relations of adolescents to family and other stress in terms of emotional and behavioural problems, and impaired self-esteem. However, a causal pattern from stress to mental health problems cannot be demonstrated beyond reasonable doubt (Bagley and Mallick 2000).

The impact on the organisation and functioning of refugee and asylum seeking families is regarded as a risk factor for the development of mental health problems in children and young people. The children of torture victims may present with high levels of emotional and anxiety states even though they themselves have not been directly exposed to these traumatic events. Similarly, while children may adapt more easily to their new environment and develop language skills, their parents may not. This can cause intergenerational tension and lead to a reduction in parental influence and authority that becomes problematic at important developmental transition points such as adolescence.

Roma, gypsy and traveller children may be included in recent groups of asylum and refugee seeking families escaping to the UK from ethnic 'cleansing' in the Balkan region of Central and Eastern Europe; other groups fleeing political or religious persecution are fleeing from Africa and the Middle East to Europe; from South America and Mexico to the USA and from Asia and the Pacific to Australia.

These children and families have a long history of persecution and flight from discrimination (Kiddle 1999). In particular Roma, gypsy and traveller families who have for many years made their home in Britain are probably one of the most socially excluded groups of people living in this country (Saravanan et al. 2004). Unemployment among Roma/gypsies is in the region of 70 per cent, while increasing numbers of children are failing to complete even a basic education.

These factors, particularly the lack of proper education, are risk factors for the development of mental health problems and subsequent self-harm. The overall context of social exclusion means an absence of contact with preventive services or the positive interaction with peers necessary for developmental attainment.

Lesbian, bisexual, gay and transgender young people

Recent evidence confirms for example, that suicide is of particular concern in marginalised and victimised adolescent groups including gay, lesbian and bisexual youth. Research suggests that despite the rhetoric of anti-discriminatory policies and professional statements of equality, heterosexist and homophobic attitudes continue to be displayed by some parents, health staff, psychologists and social workers (Morrison and L'Heureux 2001).

This can further reinforce feelings of rejection, confusion and despair in troubled young people. Other evidence warns against a narrow definition of sexual-minority adolescents that pathologises their behaviour or wrongly assumes a lesser risk of self-harming behaviour.

Adolescents at risk of suicide can feel that they can resolve their internal states of despair and angst by splitting away from their body. Thus by killing their physical body they believe they can liberate their psychic self from the emotional pain and suffering. Adolescents at risk of psychosis are often suicidal, but suicide is not the outcome in many cases.

Working with adolescents who are suicidal means being exposed to intense and extreme emotions such as anxiety, guilt, responsibility and fear. It is highly problematic to work with because it is immune to predictability and because there are multiple aspects to suicidality (Briggs 2002).

Models of self-harm

Having a theory of self-harm is helpful for some people – it can help make sense of or explain something which seems extraordinary, mysterious and perplexing. Three main models of self-harm are currently being considered and are subject to research. They are biological, environmental and psychological.

In modern practice among doctors, social workers, nurses, psychologists and therapists, no one theory can offer an explanation of why young people in particular self-harm in increasing numbers. It's more complex and likely to be an interplay between all three factors and the way they can influence or even reinforce each other.

Biological factors

It is likely that low levels of the hormone serotonin which regulates impulsivity and mood may be associated with self-harm by lowering mood and reducing young people's ability to regulate impulsivity.

Endorphins and enkephalins are known to be released when young people self-harm. These chemicals produce feelings of euphoria and stress relief. Also, some young people may be able to produce pain reducing chemicals which may increase their pain threshold.

A decrease in serotonin levels may also trigger self-directed aggression, while any impairment in the dopamine system, caused by head injury trauma, is believed to be associated with repetitive self-harm.

High levels of serotonin and positive, supportive parental relationships are protective against self-harm, as is good bonding and attachment with a new born infant who if neglected and poorly attached will have raised cortisol levels which are a predictor of future self-harm.

Psychological factors

As we have mentioned earlier, thoughts of self-criticism, low self-esteem and hopelessness are common in young people who self-harm; these thoughts are associated with feelings of depression, anxiety or heightened arousal.

Paradoxically the act of self-harm is reported by young people to improve their mood, release tension and decrease intolerable emotional pain. This is hard for parents and professionals to grasp, so the important thing is to be aware of the psychological state of a young person which can worsen or lessen the likelihood of self-harm.

Environmental factors

As we noted earlier, the development of children and young people is influenced greatly by their immediate and wider environment. This is not to say that only deprived young people from poor families or impoverished neighbourhoods self-harm. On the contrary young people who self-harm come from all classes and cultures.

The key factor is in the relationship with their parents. Cold, dismissive, preoccupied and self-absorbed parents can be rich or poor and create the emotional environment that fosters the conditions where the risk of self-harm increases.

Parents also model emotions and behaviour that can be learned and internalised by the developing child. So a parent who has mental health problems, or who manages stress poorly or is subject to self-destructive acts will be creating the foundations for a repetition in their child to be more likely.

On the other hand parents who can be open about feelings and positive ways to manage them, or who pay close attention to a young person's mood, or who can demonstrate problem-solving skills, can mitigate the likelihood of self-harm.

Myths about self-harm

Adults who encounter self-harm in young people and others can quickly react according to powerful beliefs that have built up over time regarding this problem. These myths are enduring and probably influence many parents and professionals who are in a state of shock and disbelief when they first realise that a young person, for example, is self-harming.

The young person is just attention-seeking

In fact evidence strongly suggests that deliberate self-harm is done for the opposite reasons. It is usually a private act which is concealed and not disclosed to friends or family by young people with low self-esteem who because of the stigma attached to self-harm are unlikely to seek help. The last thing they want is for attention from anyone.

Self-harm does not really hurt

It is also important to remember that every person has a different pain threshold. However, cutting or other acts of deliberate self-harm does hurt although the initial pain sensation may be blunted by the intense emotions or associated drug and alcohol use. It seems that the sense of pain is very high by the time the young person is receiving treatment.

The seriousness of the problem is associated with the severity of the injury

There is no evidence to support this proposition. A young person who self-harms in a minor way by superficial cutting may be feeling just as sad, depressed or suicidal as the young person who takes a serious overdose.

Only teenaged girls self-injure

Research (Bagley and Mallick 2000) over the past five years demonstrates that members of both genders, from six continents, and ranging in age from 14–60+ reported self-harming.

Self-inflicted violence is just an attempt to manipulate others

Some people use self-inflicted injuries as an attempt to cause others to behave in certain ways. Most don't, though. It's more important to focus on what it is they want and how you can communicate about it while maintaining appropriate boundaries. Look for the deeper issues and work on those.

Recognising and Treating Self-Harm

The professional context

Part of the real problem with dealing with self-harm and risk of suicide for professionals working with children and young people is to be able to fit the phenomenon into their existing core training and working context.

Nurses, social workers, teachers, youth workers and others will have had minimal training or knowledge about self-harm and suicide risk. Indeed a recent report from the Royal College of General Practitioners in the UK admitted that GP training in this area is almost non-existent (DoH 2003). Initial teacher, social work and nurse training also have minimal child and adolescent mental health content in their curricula.

The problem is further compounded by the lack of training in general available to all professional staff and others working with children and young people (CAMHS Review 2008). And then there is the wider context of public attitudes, political willingness, and cultural pressures to avoid recognising the extent of mental health problems in society in general and in particular among young people. There is enormous prejudice against people suffering with depression and anxiety problems – partly because they are invisible health problems, unlike a cancer patient or road accident victim or a disabled soldier returning from war fighting duties.

Defining problems

The picture is further complicated by theoretical differences and epidemiological evidence about the aetiology of mental health problems, its causes and manifestations. This leads to differences between professionals about how to define mental illness or certain categories of illness, some of which are misunderstood, such as schizophrenia, or the subject of controversy, such as attention deficit hyperactive disorder in young people.

If it is problematic to define mental illness or disorder, then it is equally difficult to define what is meant by mental health – especially for children and young people who evolve and grow quickly in their adolescent years and experience intense emotions, which can be mistaken for early signs of potential self-harm and suicidal intent. It can mean different things to families, children, or professionals, and staff from different professional backgrounds might not share the same perception of what mental health is. Mental health in childhood and adolescence is indicated by:

- a capacity to enter into and sustain mutually satisfying personal relationships

- a continuing progression of psychological development

- an ability to play and to learn so that attainments are appropriate for age and intellectual level

- a developing moral sense of right and wrong

- the degree of psychological distress and maladaptive behaviour being within normal limits for the child's age and context.

Defined in this way, mental health is a rather ideal state, which depends upon the potential and experience of each individual, and is maintained or hindered by external circumstances and events (Mental Health Foundation 1999). According to one definition the child who is mentally healthy, 'will obviously be both efficient and successful, for all his energies are employed to their full capacity. He will have a strong will and character, and be intelligent and moral' (Hadfield 1975). This rather dated, and telling, minimalist definition which illustrates something of the value base and perceptions of contemporary psychiatric practice, can be contrasted with a more fulsome modern definition suggesting that children who are mentally healthy will have the ability to:

- develop psychologically, emotionally, creatively, intellectually and physically

- initiate, develop and sustain mutually satisfying personal relationships

- use and enjoy solitude

- become aware of others and empathise with them

- play and learn

- develop a sense of right and wrong

- resolve (face) problems and setbacks and learn from them.

None of the above rule out the chance that such a young person is immune from self-harm or suicide, which can be triggered suddenly, without any pre-disposing warning signs. Mental health is also described as: 'a relative state of mind in which a person... is able to cope with, and adjust to, the recurrent stress of everyday living' (Kurtz, Thomas and Wolkind 1995).

This definition of mental health introduces the idea of relativity and seems to advance the notion of coping with and adjusting to everyday living. Do black children and young people have to cope with and adjust to the everyday stress of racism? Can mental health be achieved by tolerating unemployment, poor housing, or social exclusion? Some professional staff will be attuned to the social dimension affecting children's mental health. They need to consider how they define the terms mental disorder and mental health and whether their practice aims to help children and young people 'adjust to the stress of everyday living' or challenge those stresses within a personal helping relationship which can help prevent self-harm or potential suicide.

The link with child and adolescent mental health

These definitions and the subtle distinctions between mental illness and mental health are important in the sense that they set the context for how parents and others conceptualise self-harm experienced by children and young people.

The role of health managed child and adolescent mental health services (CAMHS 2008) is important in this context because we know that formal clinical services are underused by young people who prefer more open, accessible user-friendly help and support (Walker 2003a).

Examples later on in this text will illustrate how education, youth justice, and social work staff can all offer quite different explanations for the same behaviour with significantly different outcomes to intervention. So it is very important to be as clear as you can be about what it is you are observing and what sources of knowledge are informing those perceptions.

Labelling a troubled teenager as anti-social, aggressive and moody could also be a description of someone who is likely to begin to self-harm and proceed towards suicide (Rowan 2001). Acquiring a label of mental illness can not only be stigmatising in the short term but can have profound longer term consequences for a young person in terms of relationships, employment, education and personal health or life insurance.

A nationwide survey of child mental health discovered that children under 15 years of age with obsessive-compulsive disorder were going undetected and failing to receive appropriate help despite the availability of safe and effective treatment (ONS 2007). Further evidence for the difference in professional perceptions of mental health problems is shown by another survey conducted among local family doctors. It revealed that they were only identifying 2 per cent of the 23 per cent of children attending local surgeries who had some form of severe psychological or emotional problem (Walker 2003a).

These findings are worrying because primary care is one of the most crucial gateways for children and young people to gain access to appropriate services and resources and for signposting to accessible and acceptable support in this area. They ought to be places where early warning signs of self-harm are detected and acted upon.

Child and adolescent development

Understanding the key elements of human growth and development theoretical resources relevant to child and adolescent development are critical to parents and professionals seeking to assess and intervene appropriately in the lives of troubled young people who may self-harm. Summaries have been assembled below. They have been simplified to aid clarity and comparison and should be seen as part of a wide spectrum of potential, rather than deterministic, interactive causative factors in the genesis of self-harm and potential suicide.

TABLE 2.1 SUMMARY OF DEVELOPMENTAL CONCEPTS

Theory	Age range	
	6–11	12–18
Eriksen's psycho-social stages of development	The older child begins to acquire knowledge and skills to adapt to surroundings. Develops sense of achievement but marred by possible feelings of inferiority and failure if efforts are denigrated	The individual enters a stage of personal and vocational identity formation. Self-perception heightened, but potential for conflict, confusion and strong emotions. These can escalate in certain situations such as bullying, parental conflict, abuse leading to self-harm
Freud's psychosexual stages of development	The latency stage, which is characterised by calm after the storm of the powerful emotions preceding it	The genital stage whereby the individual becomes interested in opposite-sex partners as a substitute for the opposite-sex parent, and as a way of resolving the tensions inherent in oedipal and electra complexes. But where a parent has overtly or covertly favoured a child or rejected them the resulting anguish can be turned inwards to self-harm
Bowlby's attachment theory	The main carer's absences become longer, but the child develops a reciprocal attachment relationship	The child and developing young person begins to understand the carer's needs from a secure emotional base. But where a secure base has not formed due to emotional neglect, deprivation, or parental mental illness – the risk of self-harm increases
Piaget's stages of cognitive development	This stage is characterised by less egocentric thinking and more relational thinking–differentiation between things. The complexity of the external world is beginning to be appreciated	The stage of formal operations characterised by the use of rules and problem-solving skills. The child moves into adolescence with increasing capacity to think abstractly and reflect on tasks in a deductive, logical way. But in a chaotic household, with inconsistent parenting, and a hostile social environment, a young person can resort to self-harm to resolve inner turmoil and pain

Some social psychologists criticise the emphasis in child development theories on normative concepts and suggest enhancing the judging, measuring approach towards one that embodies context, culture, and competencies. In other words don't be too influenced by the idea of what is 'normal' because they can stop you seeing the individual child and their characteristics, unique personality and strengths which will lead you to think creatively about helping them (Woodhead 1998). Crucially, a better understanding of developmental processes can help professionals identify those points of stress and pressure where young people are more vulnerable to self-harm.

Adolescent well-being

Adolescence is acknowledged to be an under-researched area of child and adolescent mental health development.

Service provision for this age range of young people is poor (Schoon *et al.* 2002). It therefore warrants particular attention. A research study looked at the mental health of adolescents in the UK over the past 25 years, and found that adolescent emotional problems (such as depression and anxiety) have increased for both girls and boys since the mid-1980s. Adolescent conduct problems showed a continuous rise for both boys and girls over the whole 25-year study period.

'The strength of associations between these problems and poor outcomes later in adulthood have remained similar over time... and are not the result of an increasing tendency for parents to rate teenagers as problematic, but the result of real changes in problem levels' (ONS 2007, p.66). These are the pre-conditions that can provoke a vulnerable young person into self-harm and potential suicide.

Marked changes in family type (such as increases in the numbers of single-parent families) over the period were not the main reason for rising trends in behaviour problems, and changes in socio-economic indicators were not the main reason either, although there is now a social class gradient in emotional difficulties that was not there before.

A further research study also observed that, while studies from, for example, the Netherlands and the US have shown either no increase, or even recent decreases in levels of psychosocial difficulties, the trend has continued upwards in the UK (Ingham 2008).

Why is it important to promote adolescent well-being?

In the short term interrupting poor mental health as soon as possible in the childhood and adolescent years will reap instant rewards for young people. Those who are supported and have more positive mental health can learn better and are more likely to fulfil their social, academic and training potential. It is likely that intervening more effectively and imaginatively could significantly reduce adolescent mortality (through reducing suicide rates) and improve life experiences.

If we can accurately assess mental health problems, and we know both how to intervene and also that a particular intervention may work, then there is an ethical imperative to do something as soon as we can.

Enhancing health and educational outcomes will benefit young people in the shorter term by potentially reducing self-harm, but will of course benefit all of us in the longer term as well. A significant proportion of young people with mental health problems will go on to be adults with not just ongoing mental health problems, but also a range of other poor outcomes as well – difficulties with relationships, unstable employment histories, involvement in crime, and social exclusion.

These all have enormous financial and social consequences. Research has shown that by age 28, people with continuing high levels of anti-social behaviour have cost society up to 10 times more than those with no problems – these are the costs of public services such as extra educational provision, foster and residential care, and unemployment benefits, quite apart from the personal costs to the individual. The young person who fails to access appropriate help and support early enough is at greater risk of self-harm and suicide as an adult (Walker 2010).

Methods and models of practice

The following methods and models of practice are not unique to modern practice nor are they an exclusive list. Within each are specific skills sets informed by sound theory and research. They have been chosen from the classic historical texts embracing the range of modern methods and models available to aid clarity in selection of the most appropriate components of an effective intervention in working with young people who self-harm.

Discussion of the merits of defining methods and models of work and examination of the distinctions between terms such as practice approach, orientation and perspective, has been resisted for the sake of brevity and in order to avoid adding to the confusion already highlighted in the literature or to be too prescriptive about what helps. However, in reality the practitioner and the young person/family will evolve their own unique ways of managing and resolving the problem, probably by using an eclectic mix of methods and practice skills.

Crisis intervention

Crisis intervention has become a practice with a theoretical base and can be identified by certain characteristics (Caplan 1961). It is pre-eminently the approach that most professionals will use when attending to a young person who has self-harmed or attempted suicide. Drawing on psychodynamic principles it is aimed at strengthening the child's internal psychological resources through a personal relationship within which you can positively reinforce their coping strategies. Crisis theory is described as a time when a person finds themselves much more dependent upon external sources of support than at other times in their life. It has been described as having three distinct phases:

1. Impact – recognising a threat.

2. Recoil – attempting to restore equilibrium but failing, leaving the person feeling stressed and defeated.

3. Adjustment/adaptation or breakdown – when the person begins to move to a different level of functioning.

It is usually a set of interrelated factors and triggers that produce a state of crisis, such as self-harm, some of which can be anticipated while others cannot. Rather than see crises as individual failure it is better to think of them as opportunities for interventions when the young person is more likely to respond. Characteristics include:

- helps the young person gain insight into their functioning and better ways of coping

- used in conjunction with risk assessment and risk management techniques

- is usually short-term in nature

- relates a young person's internal crises to external changes

- can help in case of loss, bereavement, reactive depression and trauma

- based on the idea that people can return to a previous level of functioning.

DISADVANTAGES

Crisis intervention may be used as the default setting for modern practice as government and employers re-define modern public support services to a reactive service administering problems, gatekeeping resources and referring clients on to other services. Done well it offers opportunities for advanced, reflective, psycho-social practice and high levels of interpersonal skill. But if it is used to ration, exclude and constrain then it is more a mechanism of social control.

Community work practice

Helping people within their own communities is endorsed by valid research as better than removing them to unfamiliar surroundings (Okitikpi and Aymer 2008). In terms of self-harm this is part of a preventative strategy targeted at individuals or communities at high risk.

The theoretical base of such practice is political and socialist in origins. In its narrowest definition it might exclude statutory work and identify it with voluntary, non-statutory sector staff engaged in pressure group action or outreach activity (Henderson and Thomas 1987).

A broader definition would include it as part of the repertoire of skills required in progressive practice. It is characterised by partnership, anti-discriminatory, empowering practice aimed at reducing social exclusion and fostering self-help. It comprises these specific skills:

- galvanising
- focusing
- clarifying
- summarising
- gatekeeping

- mediating

- informing.

DISADVANTAGES

Young people who are homeless or in crisis are not often linked to their neighbourhoods, kinship networks or informal support; therefore it is difficult to galvanise them or enable them to accept help offered.

The community itself may be hostile to them and their behaviours as well as reflecting racist beliefs and discriminatory practices. These are all danger signs for tipping a desperate young person into self-harming behaviour. Institutional organisation of modern health and social practice is part of the structure of society and welfare which has let many young people down.

Systemic practice

Employing a systemic or systems model in child and adolescent mental health practice will be characterised by the key notion that individual children and young people have a social context which will be influencing to a greater or lesser extent, their behaviour and their perception of their problem (Minuchin 1974).

An important social context is that of the family and this has led to the practice of family therapy as a method of practice. It is often the case that in cases of self-harm or suicide attempt the young person is acting as a sentinel for a broader family problem which might relate to domestic violence, adultery, adult mental illness, or constant parental conflict.

It offers a broad framework for intervention enabling the mapping all of the important elements affecting families as well as a method of working with those elements to reduce the likelihood of repeated self-harm. Key features include:

- convening family meetings to give voice to everyone connected to an individuals problem (e.g. family group conference)

- constructing a geneogram (family tree) with a family to help identify the quality of relationships

- harnessing the strengths of families to support individuals in trouble

- using a problem-oriented style to energise the family to find their own solutions

- assisting in the development of insight into patterns of behaviour and communication within the family system

- adopting a neutral position as far as possible in order to avoid accusations of bias/collusion.

Many professionals use this model as an overarching framework to help guide their practice. It is particularly useful to use to clarify situations where there is multi-agency and multi-professional involvement in clients' lives. It can help the drawing of boundaries and sort out who does what in often complex, fast-moving, and confusing situations. It also helps avoid the assumption that the individual child or young person is necessarily the main focus for intervention, which is invariably what happens in cases of self-harm.

DISADVANTAGES

It can be difficult for some families to appreciate the interconnectedness of the problems of individual children with wider influences. There is a natural tendency to focus on the young person at the centre of attention when they have self-harmed, rather than to adopt a wider perspective. It is a way of viewing the position, role and behaviour of various individuals within the context of the whole system, but in so doing appear abstract, culturally insensitive, and disempowering. Used uncritically it can negate the importance of individual work, as well as avoiding location of responsibility in child abuse situations.

Psycho-dynamic practice

The model offers a concept of the mind, its mechanisms, and a method of understanding why some children behave in seemingly repetitive, destructive ways.

It is the essential one-to-one helping relationship involving advanced listening and communication skills (Hughes 1999). It provides a framework to address profound disturbances and inner conflicts within children and adolescents around issues of loss, attachment, anxiety, and personal development which can lead to self-harm.

Key ideas such as defence mechanisms, and the transference in the relationship between worker and client, can be extremely helpful in reviewing the work being undertaken, and in the process of supervision.

The model helps evaluate the strong feelings aroused in particular work situations, where for example a client transfers feelings and attitudes onto the worker that derive from an earlier significant relationship. The worker will actually experience feelings of anger, self-loathing, futility and guilt when working intensely with a young person who has self-harmed and has suicidal ideas.

Counter-transference occurs when the worker tries to live up to that expectation and behave for example, like the client's parent in a judgmental, critical or compliant way towards the young person's demands. Key features include:

- It is a useful way of attempting to understand seemingly irrational behaviour.

- The notion of defence mechanisms is a helpful way of assessing male adolescents who have difficulty expressing their emotions.

- It acknowledges the influence of past events/ attachments and can create a healthy suspicion about surface behaviour.

- The development of insight can be a particularly empowering experience to enable children and young people to understand themselves and take more control over their own lives.

- The model has influenced a listening, accepting approach that avoids over-directiveness.

- It can be used to assess which developmental stage is reflected in the child or young person's behaviour and to gauge the level of anxiety/depression.

DISADVANTAGES

The conventional criticisms of this model are its genesis in a medical model of human behaviour that relies on expert opinion without too much account of the person in their socio-economic context.

In its original, uncritical form it pathologises homosexuality and negates gender power relationships. This is of concern when dealing with a young person whose self-harm is based around their confused sexuality, homosexual urges, or resistance to comply with stereotypical gendered 'norms'.

It is not considered an appropriate way of working with some ethnic minority groups and on its own cannot adequately explain the effects of racism. However, modern practitioners have adapted the original model to embrace diversity and cultural factors and are able to incorporate a more humanistic approach to teenage sexuality that does not discriminate against homosexual/bisexual or transgendered identities.

Cognitive behavioural practice

Practice with this model is based on the key concept that all behaviour is learned and therefore available to be unlearned or changed.

It offers a framework for assessing the pattern of behaviour in children and adolescents and a method for altering their thinking, feeling, and behaviour (Bandura 1986). The intervention can be used with individuals and groups of young people. It is becoming the most prevalent model of therapeutic intervention in conventional health care provision and the one most likely to be offered to a young person who has self-harmed. It aims to help them become aware of themselves, link thoughts and emotions, and enable them to acquire new life skills.

Using this approach you would decide on the goals/new behaviours to be achieved with the client, those that are clear but also capable of measurement. The four major behavioural techniques include desensitisation, aversion therapy, operant conditioning and modelling. Key features include:

- using the ABC formula – what are the Antecedents, the Behaviour and the Consequences of the problem

- focusing on what behaviours are desired and reinforcing them

- modelling and rehearsing desired behavioural patterns

- combining behavioural and cognitive approaches to produce better results

- gradually desensitising a child or young person to a threat or phobia.

Behavioural approaches have appeal for staff undertaking intervention because they offer a systematic, scientific approach from which to structure their practice. The approach goes some way towards encouraging participatory practice, discouraging labelling, and maintains the client's story as central.

The idea of 'learned helplessness' has the potential to bridge the gap between psychological and sociological explanations of behaviour, maintaining the focus on both social and individual factors.

DISADVANTAGES

Usually it is only the immediate environment of the child that is examined. It is not as value-free as it claims. The scientific nature of behavioural assessment rests on modernist assumptions about certainty. There is often in practice a tendency to rush a solution after a limited assessment where the theory is bent so that the individual client changes to accommodate their circumstances rather than the other way round. The potential to use the theory to employ anti-oppressive practice is limited because much of the theory is based on white, male, western norms of behaviour.

Task-centred practice

Task-centred work is often cited as the most popular base for contemporary assessment and intervention practice in social work for example, but it may be that it is used as a set of activities rather than as a theoretically-based approach from which a set of activities flows (Doel and Marsh 1992). Key features include:

- It is based on client agreement or service user acceptance of a legal justification for action.

- It aims to move from problem to goal, from what is wrong to what is needed.

- It is based around tasks which are central to the process of change and which aim to build on individual service user strengths as far as possible.

- The approach is time-limited, preserving client self-esteem and independence as far as possible.

- It is a highly structured model of practice using a building block approach so that each task can be agreed and success or not measured by moving from problem to goal.

It can serve as a basic approach for the majority of children and young people who self-harm. In this approach the problem is always the problem as defined by the client. It therefore respects their values, beliefs and perceptions. This approach encourages children and young people to select the problem they want to work on and engages them in task selection and review.

It lends itself to a collaborative and empowering approach by enabling you to carry out your share of tasks and review them alongside the clients'. Time limits and task reviews aid motivation and promote optimism.

DISADVANTAGES

Although this approach has the capacity for empowerment, it can sometimes prohibit active measures by practitioners to ensure it does.

Although ostensibly value-free and intrinsically non-oppressive, you should continually reflect on your practice to make this explicit. The coaching role could be open to abuse, or permit you to become overly directive. The emphasis on simple, measurable tasks may focus attention on concrete solutions that obscure the potential advocacy role of practice.

The approach requires a degree of cognitive ability and motivation in the child or young person that in some cases will be lacking in very depressed young people prone to self-harm and suicidal thoughts.

Narrative therapeutic practice

Narrative therapeutic ideas have developed in recent years among some workers captivated by the notion of storytelling as a means to engage children and young people (Freeman, Epston and Lobovits 1997).

Perhaps this development is a reaction against the increasingly technocratic age we live in and where children are surrounded and constantly stimulated by largely visual and auditory media or communication. Storytelling is advocated by educationalists attempting to reach children in schools, theatres and libraries as a way of preserving some interest in the written word. Ethnic minority communities endeavour to use storytelling in large industrialised countries as a means of recovering their indigenous, cultural history and maintaining rituals obscured by the homogenised consumer-oriented culture offered by profiteering hegemonic corporations.

Narrative therapeutic ideas recognise the ability children and young people have to ascribe meaning to events that serve to explain but also to influence choices about the possible courses of action. This capacity to generate and evolve new narratives and stories to make sense of experiences involves the use of culturally shared myths, legends and fairy stories.

Thus therapy is seen as not just offering new perceptions and insights, but in the very nature of the conversation taking place. Narrative therapists suggest that problems are derived and maintained from the internalisation of oppressive ways of perceiving the self. This comes very close to describing the state of mind of many young people who self-harm as an act of internal self-destruction. These notions can be reinforced by parents who constantly criticise a child or who only respond negatively to behaviours.

Key characteristics include:

- The technique of externalising the problem whereby the social worker encourages the child to objectify or personify the problem outside of themselves.

- The child can separate themselves from the problem instead of being seen and related to by others as the problem.

- The child or young person is engaged in a process of exploring and resisting the problem as an unwanted impediment rather than as an integral part of their psychic constitution.

- A troubled young person is enabled to begin the process of challenging self-defeating and overwhelming negative self-concepts.

Children and young people who are suffering from psychological distress requiring therapeutic help may be either too young or too old to engage in cognitive and verbal communication about their feelings and experiences.

The young ones may be more at ease with activities and play materials to aid expression while the older teenagers will often be difficult to engage and open up, having learned the basic defence of silence. But they will all know something of fairy tales, myths and legends (Walker 2005). Every culture has them and they are usually told during early childhood in a verbal parental or carer ritual as old as time itself. Earliest school literature incorporates these stories in the education curriculum precisely because they are familiar and accessible.

As part of the healing process, literature is an often underrated asset. Yet it carries information about families, emotions, morality, relationships and so much else in a way that can enable very damaged children to use devices such as fairy stories to help understand themselves at a deeper level. Fairy stories have the capacity to capture the child's imagination because they usually involve fantastical creatures, transformational experiences or complex predicaments in which the child can immerse themselves and relate to their inner world.

DISADVANTAGES

A child's repressed feelings and worst fears cause inner conflicts that can manifest in acting out behaviour or anxiety states leading to mental health problems and self-harm specifically.

These defences may be a necessary phase through which the child needs to pass before being able to change. Impatience on your part may be unhelpful. Fairy stories operate at the overt level where concepts of right and wrong and other moral dilemmas may seem obvious to you. But the story also operates at a covert level carrying important messages to the conscious, preconscious and unconscious mind that will affect the child's sense of culture.

Risk assessment

Some young people may self-harm just once or twice. For others it can become a habitual response to any overwhelming situation. They might self-harm several times per day during difficult periods in their life. Therefore, it is important that the issue is addressed immediately and assessment is the gateway to understanding and future management.

It is rare for self-harming behaviour to exist in isolation. Self-harm often follows on from earlier problem behaviours and illustrates that an addictive quality exists across a range of behaviour.

The literature supports the view that for young women there are well-established links both with eating disorders and overdosing (Walker 2010). Any risk assessment should be able to answer the following:

- What makes the person harm themselves?

- Do they want to die when they commit the act of self-harm?

- Have they felt this way before?

- Have they had any previous help with self-injurious behaviour?

- Do they still feel like harming themselves?

- Do they want help?

Your risk assessment needs to be directed to four main issues: assessment and management of the current episode; identification and management of associated problems; identification and promotion of the child and family's resources; and prevention of repetition.

Initial steps

All young people who have self-harmed should receive prompt medical attention. Intent should be assessed.

Workers need to obtain sequential details about the events that occurred in the 48 hours preceding the act of self-injury and explore circumstances surrounding the act or planned act: the reasons, the method, the degree of planning, the location of the act, the presence of a suicide note, the expected extent of injury, any actions after the attempt, whether drugs were consumed (prescribed or illicit), the likelihood of being stopped in time or revived, the extent of the desire to die, feelings about living.

It is essential that workers establish any previous acts of self-injury as well as trying to establish the young person's behaviour before, during and after the incident, and on any major life events they may recently have experienced.

Identifying other problems

Work with the young person to devise a list of the most important current problems. Self-harm in young people is associated with depression, drug or alcohol abuse, behavioural problems, and physical illness.

There is often an association with family difficulties, including parental discord and violence, parental depression or substance abuse, role models of self-harming behaviour in the family, abuse of all kinds, and bereavement.

Other associated problems include bullying at school, peer role models of self-harm, models of self-harm in the media, and educational difficulties. Some young people who self-harm have associated mental health problems and so it is important to look for evidence of major depression, anxiety, psychotic or paranoid symptoms, misuse of alcohol or illicit drugs or withdrawal (especially withdrawal from amphetamines or cocaine).

Promoting the child and family's resources

Factors in the child that protect them from self-harm, or from repetition of self-harm include:

- being particularly good at something (e.g. a sport)
- positive peer relationships
- good school attendance and academic achievement
- positive plans for the future.

Family factors that reduce the risk of self-harm include:

- a close relationship with at least one positive role model

- parenting styles that encourage rather than punish

- clear methods for communication within the family.

Coping resources, for example, family, friends also need to be examined. Access to appropriate coping resources reduces the risk of self-injury and of suicide. Your role may focus on increasing the number of appropriate coping resources and consider who else should be involved, such as friends, relatives and external organisations.

Preventing repetition

This should begin with an assessment of the risk factors for frequent repetition since motivations for self-harming behaviour change over time and context.

Assessment of mental state and continuing intent to self-harm will usually require that the young person be interviewed without the parent. There is no evidence that encouraging children and young people to talk with professionals about their feelings and plans precipitates self-harm (Calder 2007).

Factors suggesting there is continuing intent include:

- a clear statement that the young person intends to harm themselves again (such a statement should always be taken seriously)

- depression

- unresolved personal or family problems (particularly if these appeared to precipitate previous self-harm)

- hopelessness

- clear plans to self-harm

- easy access to dangerous methods

- frequent previous attempts.

Assessing the level of risk

Marfe (2003) identified four very useful risk categories to help social workers analyse the information they have collected, which are detailed below.

Four useful risk categories

THE YOUNG PERSON AT EXTREMELY HIGH RISK

This young person has made previous attempts at serious self-harm, indicated clear intentions of a wish to die and has made a deliberate premeditated suicide attempt.

The young person will have obtained the agent (tablets, etc.) prior to the day of attempt and believes the agent or themselves will cause significant harm. They will have specifically arranged a time when he or she reckons they will to be alone.

They will usually have left a note regreting they were unsuccessful on the first attempt and appear to be extremely depressed or despondent.

THE YOUNG PERSON AT HIGH RISK

This young person has tried to seriously self-harm or made a suicide attempt that was planned and gave clear reasons for their actions which still pose a risk.

They will have deliberately bought the agent that day, or previously and will be aware that the agent was harmful.

They will usually leave a note, be alone when the attempt is made and still be experiencing suicidal feelings. They will be regretful or uncertain about the failed attempt at serious self-harm and appear extremely depressed.

THE YOUNG PERSON AT MODERATE RISK

This young person will have a history of deliberate self-harm, risk-taking or impulsive behaviour, and a history of poor stress coping mechanisms, but has no clear intention or a wish to seriously self-harm.

They can give clear reasons for their actions – but they no longer pose an obvious risk. They may have made an attempt to deliberately self-harm, but with no actual suicide intent.

The young person will have obtained the agent impulsively that day but was not fully aware of the effects of the overdose.

Any attempt at self-harm would have been made while others were in the vicinity and they may have informed others of their actions. The young person is glad they did not die, but may still be considering other forms of self-harm.

THE YOUNG PERSON AT LOW RISK

This young person has no history of previous deliberate self-harm or risk-taking behaviour, no history of poor stress coping mechanisms, and has no intentions of, or a wish to, seriously self-harm.

They can give clear reasons for their actions which were never intended to pose a risk and have made the self-harm actions known to others appropriately. Any accomplished self-harm occurs when others are in the vicinity or they are not planning self-harm of any kind.

Self-harm as a form of control

One of the things that self-harm offers young people is a way to feel in control of something in their lives. Even those young people who speak directly to an adult feel that once they had done this, all decision making and control were taken from them. They were not being consulted about the services that might be contacted, or about the exact sort of help and information that would support and help them deal with their self-harm.

Many were unsure – and felt unable to ask about – who else would be told or involved after they had disclosed private and sensitive information. Young people say (Truth Hurts 2006) that lack of control exacerbates the self-harm. It is also apparent that many young people who self-harm are afraid that the only coping strategy that has been keeping them functioning might be taken away from them:

> My friend went on to tell my head of year who in turn said it was necessary to inform my mother. I felt as though I had no say in what was happening and I felt out of control. Thus the self-harm increased. My mother was shocked and forced me to go to the doctors the next day. My doctor looked at me differently once I told her why I was there. It was as if I were being annoying and wasting her time. She saw my arm and told me that it was only superficial and that she would make enquiries as to what should be done with me.

> The one time I trusted them enough to tell them I had cut myself again, they rang my mother then and there. It made me hate being there even more, and I lied and lied and told them I didn't even consider it whenever I got angry anymore when truthfully it was so much in my mind, and the fact I had been so restricted in cutting myself I was actually now obsessed with it.
>
> (Truth Hurts 2006, p.53)

Fear of losing control and not being consulted with fully and appropriately about decisions in their lives are not the only barriers to disclosure.

Evidence shows that most young people do not have anyone they feel they can talk to about this private and sensitive issue, apart from their immediate friends and they certainly do not know how they might be able to contact more formal support services. In addition, they may be worried that if they do disclose their self-harm, their choices for the future may be compromised.

Anecdotal evidence from young people shows that they worry that they will not be able to work in professions such as teaching, nursing, or childcare because of the public perception that people who self-harm are 'dangerous' and should not be allowed to work with children.

Internet use and self-harm

Even if the young person does not indicate that they have internet friends with whom they talk, questions by professionals intended to assess effects of internet involvement on offline behaviour are warranted if he or she spends time at self-harm focused websites.

Questions such as the following may be useful.

- Do you have internet friends with whom you talk about self-injury?

- Do you ever take their advice?

- Can you provide examples of advice you got from an internet friend that you used?

Periodic assessment of internet use as therapy progresses is also warranted in young people where self-harm focused internet use is common. A professional could ask the young person to record their use of such websites and how this use affected them in terms of a 'comfort' scale:

extremely   extremely
uncomfortable   comfortable

```
 1     2     3     4     5     6     7     8     9    10
 L__ _I__ _I__ _I__ _I__ _I__ _I__ _I__ _I__ _J
```

The trigger, nature, and duration of any impulses to injure while on a particular site should also be recorded.

Because internet use, in and of itself, can become habit forming – what some have called 'internet addiction' – it is very important in contemporary society for professionals to understand where such activity helps or hinders young people who self-harm (Whitlock, Lader and Conterio 2007).

Suggesting trying to collect information on self-injury internet use is significantly easier than issuing recommendations about how that information is used. At the most basic level, online friendships and communities ought to be accorded similar regard as parallel offline relationships which can involve mutual support or very destructive bullying, or even encouragement to self-harm and attempt suicide.

For those who practise self-injury behaviours, it may be a means of expressing suppressed feelings and of connecting with others like themselves. Because self-expression and healthy connection are critical components of recovery, the internet may have a productive and effective place in treatment.

These very qualities, however, also make the internet a potentially dangerous place for self-harming individuals who use online experiences as a substitute for development of offline skills and relationships. Contemporary professionals in the meantime need to ensure they assess the quantity, quality, and nature of internet use in treating self-harming young people.

CHAPTER 3

Early Intervention, Prevention and the Journey to Recovery

Immediate help and support

If you discover a young person who has recently self-harmed and needs immediate medical assistance, your nearest Accident and Emergency (A&E) or Emergency Room/Department is the first place to go to.

Each year, around 25,000 admissions to hospitals in England and Wales are made by young people who have self-harmed. All hospitals now have guidelines in place for dealing with young people who self-harm in order to make the environment as supportive and comfortable as possible.

This means that when they arrive they should be given the same amount of respect, care and compassion as any patient (www.selfinjury.org.uk). Unfortunately evidence suggest this is not always the case and young people report hostility, anger or indifference from medical staff who admit experiencing punitive attitudes (Walker and Becket 2011).

If the young person needs medical attention it's crucial to ensure they get themselves checked out. Young people can learn to tend to some minor wounds personally as part of their secretive behaviour, but if you believe they have hurt themselves badly, call an ambulance or take them to the nearest hospital.

If they have taken an overdose you should always take them to the emergency department. If they have cut themselves superficially (not fully penetrated the top layer of skin) give the wound a good clean with soapy water. If it's very deep, you feel it might need stitches or is bleeding excessively, go directly to A&E. Not every hospital has an A&E department; some hospitals have minor injury units that can deal with cuts and bruises, but usually wouldn't treat someone who came in by ambulance.

The most important factor is your attitude as a professional. Your own feelings of revulsion and anger need to be contained while you are projecting a calm, serious, non-judgemental attitude (NICE 2004).

The primary aim of an A&E department is to ensure the physical injuries are dealt with as soon as possible. When the young person arrives, a 'triage' assessment will be made to determine how critical the physical injuries and state of mind are. These are categorised as 'minor' or 'major', with the most life-threatening prioritised. The young person will either be directed to a bed or asked to wait in the waiting area.

Cutting

- The doctor will ask what has happened, what they cut themselves with; when, where and why they did this.

- You and the young person will be asked if there is a history of mental illness. As the physical injury is only one part of the emergency, this needs to be known so the young person can be suitably cared for.

- The wounds will be cleaned and the doctor will look to see how deep the cuts are and the muscles tested for strength and nerves. If the wound isn't very deep and there doesn't seem to be any nerve or muscle damage, it can be closed with paper stitches or medical glue.

- If the wound is particularly deep, a local anaesthetic to numb the area can be given.

- If there is damage to the nerves and muscles, the young person may be referred to a specialist, such as an orthopaedic surgeon or plastic surgeon. They may perform an operation, which is usually done the same or following day.

Self-poisoning and overdosing

Sometimes ambulance staff may need to give your client treatment before they reach the emergency department. Depending on individual circumstances:

- The doctor will need to know what was taken, when and how much.

- Within an hour of taking the overdose your cleint may be given a drink of 'activated charcoal' – a black, unpleasant-tasting drink that prevents the stomach from absorbing the poison.

- Blood tests will be taken and paracetamol levels checked. It will depend on the amounts taken as to when your client may be treated. If there's evidence to suggest a very large overdose, treatment will start immediately, otherwise they will wait to find out the levels.

- A drip treatment may be given via a cannula (a plastic tube inserted into a vein in your client's arm) and may need to remain in place for up to 24 hours.

- For some overdoses they may just need observation in the hospital, sometimes for up to 12 hours.

Some young people decide not to tell anyone, even after a quite serious overdose. Boys tend to do this more than girls.

Some eventually reveal what happened and a parent needs to think before acting on the information and seek good quality advice before involving medical or social services. The young person may refuse to attend an appointment and unless there are associated severe mental health problems, then there will be little benefit in referring formally to other agencies.

Self-disclosure to a trusted parent is a good sign and this trust needs to be cultivated and reinforced so that a dialogue is opened with a parent. A young person who doesn't feel judged or blamed or punished will more likely talk to a parent in future if they contemplate another overdose (www. youngminds.org.uk).

Wound assessment

When it is discovered that a young person is cutting themselves it is important to assess the level of severity. Superficial cutting with quick-healing scars, transient mood changes, no history of binge drinking or pronounced drug use; no history of abuse – these are all signs that a referral to other agencies may not be helpful. On the other hand, the following indicate that a referral should be considered:

- dangerous and persistent drug or alcohol abuse

- long-term history of depression

- history of sexual abuse

- evidence of overdosing or associated eating disorder.

Consent

Staff should always make sure that the young person is mentally capable of making a decision about their treatment (NICE 2004). 'Mentally capable' means that they should be able to understand the information given to them and weigh it up in order to make a decision about whether or not to have a particular treatment. However, if they are confused from the drugs or alcohol they may have taken, they might not be able to make this decision.

The fact that they have harmed themselves is not evidence on its own that they are not capable of doing so. Healthcare professionals may ask family, friends, guardians or carers about the young person's mental capacity, if necessary.

In any case, the young person should be given full information about treatments and services, both verbally and in writing, so that they can decide if they want to go ahead with them before treatment starts. Although treatment will be routinely offered for the physical consequences of self-harm, the young person has the right to decline this treatment if they are mentally capable. On the other hand, they may want to have the physical treatments offered, but not want to have a psychological assessment.

If they choose not to have a psychological assessment they should still be offered any physical treatments they may need (Fox and Hawton 2004).

If the young person is not mentally capable, staff have a responsibility to act in their best interests. If necessary, this may include making sure they get to hospital and treating them against their stated wishes.

In rare circumstances, a young person may be treated under the Mental Health Act if they have a mental health problem. Under the Mental Health Act, the doctors and nurses will always be guided by what is in their best interests. Capacity to make informed decisions may change over time. Each new treatment should be explained to the young person and their capacity reassessed.

What happens next?

Usually the young person experiences feelings of shame, guilt, anger, self-loathing and acute embarrassment. These feelings can be magnified or minimised by the attitudes of parents, relatives, friends or other professional staff.

The young person should be referred to a child and adolescent specialist whilst in hospital or a primary care setting. Unless they are exhibiting suicidal behaviour or ideas, a risk assessment will determine when and whether they are safe to return to parental or state care.

From there an urgent referral will be made to the local child and adolescent mental health service (CAMHS) for a home visit and a process will begin to assess the way forward in terms of treatment/therapy. This could be offered on a short-term outreach basis, which many young people prefer but which has cost and resource implications. Or, they may be offered longer support at a specialist CAMHS facility where a range of professionals can offer different forms of support/ therapy (ONS 2008).

Characteristics of young people who have tried to harm, hurt or kill themselves

We have acknowledged the difficulty in recognising self-harm and the uncertainty about its prevalence. However, research conducted with both parents and young people does shed some light into this area and reveals disparities between parents' and young people's perceptions which are worth considering.

In one large study of young people aged between 11 and 15 years of age (Hawton *et al.* 2002), of those who reported they had not tried to self-harm in fact 5 per cent had done so, whereas 1 per cent of parents thought their child had self-harmed. Interestingly, in those who reported that they had tried to harm themselves (about 5%) there was almost identical agreement between parent and children's perceptions. Of the 5 per cent, 60 per cent had a mental health disorder, with the most common being depression.

Most of this 5 per cent group who had self-harmed were aged above 13 years and were girls. Twenty-nine per cent lived in single parent families, 21 per cent in reconstituted families, and 50 per cent were from families where separation or divorce had been experienced. The majority lived in households where both parents worked, and 25 per cent had experienced a major financial crisis. In about 30 per cent of these families parents reported that family communication was poor especially expression of feelings and decision making (Hawton *et al.* 2002).

The researchers also tracked the group who self-harmed in terms of their use of professional support services. Sixty per cent had used educational services and of these, a third had special educational needs. Very few had made use of emergency or family health services in the past 12 months which suggests that the stigma of the problem of self-harm combined with the attitudes of health service staff deter young people from accessing this help.

Domestic violence

Stress and coping theorists suggest that it is important to understand how young people perceive and interpret stressful events in order to assess what mediates their impact. Being involved as victims or observers of domestic violence is particularly complex because it usually happens in private, is rarely reported, often not taken seriously by law enforcement agencies, or viewed as a child protection issue by social work staff who tend to focus on physical harm rather than psychological harm.

When a child is aware of violence in the family, or when verbal and physical conflict occurs between their parents/carers, children try to understand what the outcome might be and how that will affect them. For example will a parent die, or be sent to prison? They will wonder why it is happening-are they to blame? And they will want to intervene, or what if anything they should do in response.

Children's causal attributions have important implications for their emotional and behavioural reactions. Children who blame themselves for making their parents angry or causing a conflict between them will feel guilty and depressed (Vincent and Jouriles 2000). These are fertile conditions for self-harm and suicidal thoughts to propagate. This may stimulate them to try to sort out whatever led to the conflict. Young people especially might feel responsible for ending or preventing parent fights even if they do not feel they are in any way to blame. It is not unknown for young people to try to defend a parent being physically attacked and themselves suffering physical injury.

The young person will feel drawn to take sides, thus causing further internal emotional turmoil. All of these pressures and dilemmas, and ambiguities can trigger self-harm as a way of relieving the psychological pain caused by domestic violence.

Children with special needs

Staff in special schools or residential care trying to support young people with emotional and behavioural difficulties, autism or learning disabilities will witness or find skin picking, scratching, head-banging, self-biting or head punching. They might also but less frequently witness forms of self-mutilation such as body punching, hair removal, eye poking, lip chewing or nail removal.

Young people who are quite mobile may show several challenging behaviours with physical attacks on others and temper outbursts common. Special school students with associated physical disabilities, due to restricted mobility, are more likely to self-harm.

The challenge to staff and parents/carers is first to understand why the young person is self-harming. It may be a way the young person has learned to communicate, or it may indicate fear of certain social situations, or they may be in pain due to side effects of medication, menstrual pain, muscle spasms or the effects of epilepsy.

All too often parents/carers fail to see the situation from the young person's point of view. Parent/carers might make requests or give instructions which the young person finds hard to comprehend; they may favour rigid regimes; or they may insist that young people undertake activities which they find boring (Bernard 2009).

Old-fashioned ways of managing or supporting the young person tended to rely on a rigid, punitive system which could easily backfire. For example, a young person behaving aggressively in class might be excluded and made to sit in the corridor. The young person, of course, might find this soothing, quiet and restful compared to a noisy classroom. Other punishments could actually reinforce self-harming behaviour from a young person already feeling low self-esteem.

Teachers and parents can adapt more modern and thoughtful approaches to helping the young person. Behavioural outcomes are less important than the process of interaction and communication. The key technique is to follow the lead of the young person's interests and pro-social behaviour. However, the process must be mutually enjoyable and parent/carers need to be creative in developing interactive games.

These can evolve from detailed observation of the young person and then imitating the actions and noises made by them, with physical contact an essential feature of the process. As the young person comes to enjoy the games the teacher or parent/carer can introduce new ideas and actions slowly but surely, to guide the learning of new skills.

Research has shown that the incidence of self-harm can be repetitious and chronic and that the incidence and severity of self-harm is greatest among young people with retardation, autism and severe disabilities (Heslop and Macauley 2009). Physical restraint and chemical/drug options in residential settings are more often a means of managing the institution with low, unqualified staff levels, rather than supporting the young person.

For some young people these options are required in specific circumstances, but used routinely and lazily they can prevent the individual from participating in other therapeutic, social and educational activities.

Why is self-harm prevalent in young people?

Adolescence, as we noted earlier, is a period of intense biological and emotional changes in young people where their emotions are subject to large swings and behaviour can be irrational and unpredictable. They are struggling with self-identity, emerging sexuality, independence, separation from parents and enormous peer group pressures. Self-harm need not be symptomatic of a mental health problem, it could be the result of experimentation as part of identity formation and self-image. Many find it difficult to solve problems in non-destructive ways and significant numbers are suffering with depression (NICE 2005).

The impulsivity associated with much self-harm can be thought of as linked with rejection – one of the critical points of adolescent trauma. Rejection by a friend, peer or significant relationship can produce acute impatience in the young person to get rid of the resultant feelings of distress and low self-esteem.

Elements included in the internal pressures and contradictions of these dynamics include:

- *Revenge* – this is the solution to resolving the intense internal pain and suffering following rejection. Self-harming enables the young person to be triumphant when making other people such as parents or friends feel remorse.

- *Elimination* – the aim of the young person is to get rid of the painful state of internal confusion and turbulence. The idea is that by self-harming their individual integrity is preserved through expulsion of the unwanted states of mind.

- *Dicing with death* – experimentation with self-harm is a risk to see how far the act takes them in providing strong feelings of control and omnipotence. In suicidal behaviour the aim is to overcome misery, failure and despair through taking a big risk which might end tragically but will also produce an emotional high.

Common therapeutic methods

Two of the more common forms of therapy/counselling used to help people who have self-harmed are cognitive behavioural therapy (CBT) or family therapy.

These and other interventions are summarised and compared in Chapter 2. CBT is the term used to describe a range of therapies all with a very similar approach to solving problems. They focus on the thoughts, images, beliefs and attitudes that we hold and how this relates to the way we behave.

CBT is a combination of psychotherapy and behavioural therapy. Psychotherapy emphasises the importance of the personal meaning we place on things and how thinking patterns begin in childhood. Behavioural therapy pays close attention to the relationship between our problems, our behaviour and our thoughts.

How do they work?

CBT is quite complex. There are several possible theories about how it works, and clients often have their own views. It works on the fact that your thinking can affect your feelings. So, it allows you to try and make sense of small problems by breaking them into smaller parts, which allows you to see how they are connected and how they affect you (Slee *et al.* 2008). These parts are: *a situation* – a problem, event or difficult situation. From this can follow: *thoughts, emotions, physical feelings* and *actions*.

Table 3.1 shows an example of this; it has been adapted from The Royal College of Psychiatrists website (www. rcpsych.ac.uk)

CBT helps to look at things using helpful thoughts. It takes the unhelpful and often irrational thoughts like, 'He/she ignored me – they don't like me' and think about them in a more logical and rational way. 'He/she looks a bit wrapped up in themselves – I wonder if there's something wrong?' This new thinking changes the overall end feeling, leaving the young person feeling happier about themselves and less likely to resort to self-harm as a way of dealing with the situation.

The process of CBT

In general clients attend one session a week for CBT. A course of CBT will range from 6 weeks to 6 months, depending on the therapist, the client and the pace. CBT differs from other therapies because sessions have a structure, rather than the person talking freely about whatever comes to mind.

At the beginning of the therapy, the client meets the therapist to describe specific problems associated with self-harm and to set goals they want to work towards.

TABLE 3.1 MAKING SENSE OF PROBLEMS

	Helpful	Unhelpful
Situation	You're having a bad day and school/college is feeling hard going today. As you enter the canteen for lunch someone you know walks by and, apparently, ignores you	
	Keep going, slow down, stop somewhere in the canteen where it's a bit quieter	*Leave the canteen immediately and hurriedly*
Thoughts	**He/she looks a bit wrapped up in themselves – I wonder if there's something wrong?**	*He/she ignored me – they don't like me*
Emotions	**Concern for the other person**	*Low, sad and rejected*
Physical feelings	**None – feel comfortable**	*Stomach cramps, low energy, feel sick*
Actions	**Get in touch to make sure they're OK**	*Go home and self-harm*

The problems may be troublesome symptoms, such as sleeping badly, not being able to socialise with friends, or difficulty concentrating on reading or work. Or they could be life problems, such as being unhappy at school, having trouble dealing with a friend, or being in an unhappy relationship. These problems and goals then become the basis for planning the content of sessions and discussing how to deal with them (Mind 2009).

During CBT the young person will receive 'homework' between sessions. This often requires keeping a diary of their thoughts and feelings and challenging their self-critical, unrealistic thoughts and replacing them with more realistic ones. At each session they will have the chance to discuss and bring up problems from the previous week and look at how they have been feeling since the last session.

The young person will never have to do things they don't want to do and although this type of therapy is often challenging, especially in the beginning, it can be very rewarding so it is good to encourage your client to stick with it.

Family therapy

Family therapy (or systemic psychotherapy as it is often referred to) is becoming increasingly common in many parts of the world as health and social care staff recognise that an individual with problems such as self-harm can be often best supported by those close to them (Walker and Akister 2004).

This is not always the case of course and some young people who have been abused in their own homes by a close relative should not be offered family therapy. Early research into how professional staff might experience using family therapy ideas in their work with families showed the following reasons for valuing such an approach (Gorrell-Barnes 1984). Family therapy:

- offers an open model of communication and sharing

- is enjoyed by both family and worker

- moves the focus of concern from the individual to the family with positive results

- offers a realistic way of working

- is effective in problem-solving compared to other methods

- improves the quality of family life outside problem-solving.

One of the problems professionals encounter in engaging with families in a statutory context and trying to employ family therapy methods is the threat they pose to families where the prospect of relationship changes is more overwhelming than the removal and institutionalisation of one of its members.

It is possible to observe children with mental health problems increasing their symptoms during family therapy as the focus begins to shift towards other more upsetting problems hidden within the family such as a poor marital/relationship problem.

The pattern of contact with social services, for example, may have been one of child protection/child care activity requiring the use of statutory powers to intervene. This 'resistance' to change is at the heart of all therapeutic paradigms as well as family support services.

Unfortunately this can also confirm a partial systems view that an individual needs to be sacrificed or scapegoated by a dysfunctional family, rather than everyone concerned engaging in familial change. In other words the young person may feel compelled to maintain their self-harming, not realising that they are deflecting attention from other family problems (Gorell-Barnes 1998).

However, professionals can use the systemic concept of reframing the behaviour of a troubled child or young person and the family beliefs informing it as a means of illustrating the powerful protective forces at work inside families. In other words the acceptance by some individuals to being labelled as 'the problem' can be perceived as a means of protecting the family status quo.

Suggesting to a family that the child's problem behaviour is serving a protective or loving function on behalf of other members, delivers a strong message without a blaming connotation. This also testifies to the intrinsic strengths in a family who have developed such loyalty in one of their members, strengths which may have been temporarily lost sight of during the crisis.

Some professionals using this notion will find it challenging in busy teams where despite government policy directives to the contrary, the climate is one of time constraints and resource shortages where investigation and assessment are the priority. This can create a reduction in expectations and a feeling of impotence and disempowerment in the worker that is invariably conveyed to clients. The family then have to acquire the variety of labels that trigger specialist intervention such as 'in need' or 'dysfunctional' where the opportunities for building on their strengths and resourcefulness are blighted (Walker 2006). Both professional and service user are thus restricted within circumscribed roles that militate against a positive partnership engaged in problem-solving activity.

Some family centres come closer to achieving the goal of offering a resource with a range of user-focused services such as advocacy, group work, support groups, individual counselling, and couples and family therapy.

Such centres it is argued are better equipped to provide a more comprehensive service to disadvantaged users than for example, specialist child and adolescent mental health services staffed by professionals who have a narrower range of predominantly clinical skills. Family centres are less stigmatising; they tend to have active representation from service users in the way they are run and attended by clients who are motivated to attend, thus they ironically create the ideal conditions for effective therapeutic outcomes.

Case illustration

The M family were referred to your agency following a period of increasing concern about the parents' capacity to cope with multiple problems including: unemployment, financial shortages, overcrowding, husband's violent temper, female teenager self-harming by cutting her arms and school refusing. The case was allocated to a worker who made an initial assessment and then combined this with the extensive history from the case record to produce an action plan. The evidence suggested that the family had never received consistent or coherent support, but a limited service based on superficial negative risk assessments and anxieties generated by health, social work and school staff.

Commentary

Different agencies have different policies and procedures although there is meant to be consistency and conformity. These can be influenced by the degree of urgency or perceived risk by the referrer. The first response needs to be to find out who else is involved with or known to the young person and their family. Inter-agency co-operation is crucial in all work of this nature but particularly where there are signs of potential serious self-harm escalating to suicide.

The more information the better, but this requires time to collate and analyse and then to make contact to arrange an urgent inter-agency meeting/conference. Non-attenders can submit a report or their recommendations based on their perspective and understanding of the situation.

In order to make a difference and respond in another way rather than that anticipated by other people including the family themselves, the worker using a more thoughtful approach for example, could begin by discussing options with all the family members present. This in itself would be unique because previously, for various reasons, the professional staff had only met with Mrs M or their teenage daughter.

Taking the trouble to arrange a whole family meeting immediately changes the context for the worker's visit. This permits each person to voice their perception of the family situation. This sets the scene for the work to follow and ensures that everyone has a stake in the process.

There are a number of ways forward once agreement has been reached about the practical ways of addressing the problems as defined by the family. Individual contact may need to be included, especially if there are concerns about continuing self-harm. This vital one-to-one therapeutic work can provide an exclusive and confidential space for the young person to express difficult feelings and perceptions of their situation in the family, school, or community. Another worker can help in this respect with the double advantage of providing the caseworker with additional support and another resource for certain members of the family, for example, a male social worker to meet with Mr M or a health visitor to do some parent modelling with Mrs M. A family centre could be contracted to do a number of sessions with various combinations of the family system, including extended family or friends.

A time-limited period of contact with a verbal or written agreement with a proper assessment and report at the end composed in partnership with the whole family, demonstrates a different type of engagement with the M family. Using individual therapeutic techniques, systems theory and family therapy will help the workers maintain a broad perspective of the family as an interactive system, rather than focusing narrowly on individual problems. Blame and scapegoating are to be avoided and the opportunities for change must be maximised.

Nevertheless, a professional worker will need to anticipate a potential failure in this strategy and prepare for matters to worsen that require a more statutory/directive approach if risks increase and care diminishes. Thus assessment should be a regular on-going process rather than an administrative exercise to tick boxes according to bureaucratic timescales (Walker and Beckett 2011).

It is very important in situations like these for the worker/s to be punctual, reliable, conscientious and constant in their efforts to provide continuity and certainty. This will provide the basis for trust and respect to develop and provide the context to explore painful and difficult subjects together.

Early intervention

The old saying that 'prevention is better than cure' is easy to understand and almost a statement of the obvious, however in practice it is actually quite problematic. This is because as we have discussed earlier there is no one straightforward cause of self-harm that can be targeted, or one single behaviour that triggers it that can be addressed.

Public health education programmes aimed at tackling obesity or cigarette and alcohol abuse have run for decades, but with limited success. The science and research behind self-harm is underdeveloped and there are a multitude of variables and factors that can cause the conditions for a young person to begin to self-harm.

Research on child poverty ranked Britain bottom in a comparison of the current 15 European Union countries with one in six children living in poor households; the UK has a higher percentage of children living in workless households than any other EU country (Palmer 2010). In other developed and underdeveloped countries, children's needs tend to be neglected due to their perceived lower status and importance to the commercial needs of societies.

This is an important part of the equation of demand, needs, and resources when evaluating provision and your role in supporting children and young people's emotional well-being. It has long been argued that early intervention is the key to effectiveness because it stops problems getting worse before they become harder to tackle, which may result in self-harm and suicide risk (Cooper 1999; Rutter 1999; Young Minds 2001).

Parents, teachers and professionals therefore have a responsibility in advocating strongly for increased provision of emotional and psychological support and proper resources to mitigate the chances of these problems developing in the first place.

It is less costly in terms of damage to children's development, family relationships, use of scarce resources, and anti-social consequences in the long term. However, others have pointed out that the accumulated evidence for the effectiveness of early intervention programmes is not as optimistic as was once hoped. On occasion there is the possibility that such programmes can be damaging, de-skilling, and undermining of parents' confidence. This is particularly the case if parents feel coerced into attending parent education/training programmes and when the quality of staff ability is poor.

Other evidence suggests that early education interventions demonstrated that children from disadvantaged backgrounds were less at risk from developing mental health problems, self-harm, maladjustment, school failure and delinquency after participating in these programmes which were delivered in an educational context (MacFarlane and McPherson 1995). Some outcome research on primary prevention mental health programmes focused on school-based activities and concluded that positive changes were reported in social adjustment, academic performance, and cognitive skills leading to a reduction in mental health problems in young people (MacFarlane and McPherson 1995; Richardson, Partridge and Barrett 2010).

Much of the evidence supports the idea that the *location of family support* is clearly critical in engaging parents and children in the process of tackling child and adolescent mental health problems.

Schools are emerging as an acceptable and accessible non-stigmatising venue for individual or group-based activity where, for example, attached social workers and other professionals using family support methods can engage in inter-professional work. The recent policy shift in education allowing extended schools to provide a deeper and broader range of services is evidence of the realisation that children do not learn when they are struggling with trying to maintain their emotional well-being and that if schools can promote and nurture emotional well-being, then children can learn (DfES 2003). If children can learn then it is a most powerful early intervention to help prevent mental health problems progressing and resulting in self-harm.

The purpose of intervention

The growing professional and public concern in recent years about the rising trends in children's emotional and behavioural problems has prompted health and social policy responses to the growing demand for child and adolescent mental health services in the UK and elsewhere (DoH 2004).

One of the issues raised is where and how to focus limited staffing and therapeutic resources to help families in trouble. A wider issue concerns the purpose of intervention in families – what outcomes are envisaged, how to evaluate and whether it is family support or family therapy.

Family support appears in much government guidance and literature, yet receives a low priority in statutory health and social care service provision in the UK and elsewhere. This is evidenced by a mixture of increasing pressure to improve child protection investigations, retrenchment in statutory preventive services, and the encouragement of charitable and non-governmental family support services (Walker 2003b).

Meanwhile family therapy enjoys a privileged position within the international regulatory bodies and is developing a professional status distinct from its practitioner roots in social work, psychology or nursing. Therefore the professional status and client perception of both family therapy and family support are important issues to consider when dealing with self-harming young people.

Fiscal and structural changes in the funding and organisation of social and health care are thus forcing choices about where to target finite resources to help families in need. Statutory workers bemoan the lack of time to practise preventively and at the same time are unable to employ therapeutic methods once child and adolescent mental health problems arise because of the crisis-driven nature of cases which militate against establishing a safe, containing therapeutic relationship.

Thresholds for eligibility criteria to services are so restricted that only the most worrying cases with high levels of risk such as self-harm and suicide attempts tend to be accepted into statutory services. This is of particular concern when much of self-harm is hidden (McDougall 2006).

Renewed recent interest in early intervention and preventive practice in the context of reliable evidence has enabled close examination of the challenges in assessing needs and demand against resource constraints (Gilbert 2003). Within government policy changes there is a possible ambivalence about the status and priority of family support work in the UK, and noted elsewhere (Hellinckx and Williams 1997).

Family support can be perceived as something any well-meaning person or volunteer can provide while family therapy is elevated to the rarified status of advanced professionalism

(Walker and Akister 2004). Yet they are both operating in very similar domains and can use similar therapeutic concepts with parallel processes and outcomes. More importantly, the family support worker may well have considerably more success at engaging and encouraging troubled young people than the supposedly more sophisticated therapist.

This is often explained by the more accessible and user-friendly nature of community resources often organised by charitable and voluntary sector organisations. The formal CAMHS system is heavily associated with psychiatry and medicine which young people fail to engage with (Walker 2005).

Prevention strategies

As more awareness of the problem of self-harm has grown, so too has attention to developing strategies for preventing self-harm. However, trying to identify adolescents who are at risk is notoriously difficult. This is especially the case for suicidal intent.

As we discussed earlier, there is no easy way of predicting whether a young person who self-harms is going to make a serious suicide attempt. No more than 40 per cent of adolescents who commit suicide have made previous attempts. Professionals will focus on intent, lethality, precipitants and motivation to assess whether there is a high or low risk of suicide following a previous experience.

Suicidal behaviour is more often linked to a precipitant event or circumstance which has caused a personal crisis. It could have happened very quickly or been building up over a period of time. Trying to target individuals has limited success especially with helping resources being configured to reacting to problems rather than preventing them happening in the first place. Wider socio-economic factors can mitigate the effects of despair and isolation experienced by many young people. These include stable financial circumstances, stable parent relationships, access to community leisure resources, decent housing and education provision, and a safe, friendly neighbourhood. In addition there appears to be some success in public health initiatives and 'whole-school' measures that seek to create a nurturing environment and anti-bullying strategy.

There are ways to prevent self-harm among young people. Anti-bullying strategies and whole-school approaches designed to improve the general mental health and well-being of young people appear to have a positive effect, though there is no specific evidence as yet on their impact on self-harm. Evidence from young people themselves suggests that social isolation – and believing that they are the only one that has self-harmed – can be a key factor in self-harm for some. It is likely that better information for young people about self-harm would increase their understanding and might help reduce or prevent self-harm. Similarly, better awareness and understanding among parents, teachers and others who come into contact with young people is also likely to have a positive impact.

Efficacy of preventive work

A number of studies have attempted to collate the best available evidence for evaluating what is more helpful in preventing self-harm and suicide (Fox and Hawton 2004). School-based interventions which are popular especially when linked to whole-school anti-bullying campaigns, seem to have the potential for positive and negative impact.

Some young people find information helpful while others use that information to imitate suicidal behaviour or become increasingly vulnerable to hopelessness and feelings of low self-esteem. Males are particularly susceptible to this effect. Screening programmes involving direct and discrete interviewing of individuals in school who are causing concern to teachers, are proving helpful in identifying and helping those at risk of self-harm or suicide. However, these require skilled implementation, co-operation of parent/carers and proper follow-up.

Preventive work includes attempts to control the methods used and access to weapons or objects. Evidence of the effect of public health measures to reduce alcohol and substance misuse, media guidelines to encourage more responsible reporting of self-harm and suicide, and crisis hotlines or internet sites remains however, unsubstantiated.

CHAPTER 4

Supporting the Self-Harming Child

The role of parents and carers

As mentioned earlier the role of parents and other close relatives is important in determining the progress of the young person to recovery.

The crucial task for the professional involved is to closely support the parent/carers; this will empower them and restore their confidence in coping with and managing a very stressful situation. In turn, this will have a positive impact on the troubled young person.

Clear and unconditional positive support will help the troubled young person enormously and the task of the professional is to help the adults understand that their help and support for their child can be simple and uncomplicated. This support may be very simple, for example, spending time with them and listening may seem to the parent/carer as though they are not doing anything (Walker and Akister 2004). In fact being present, available and calm will help the young person much more than being intrusive, questioning and directive.

How you react can inhibit or promote vital learning from the experience and lead to the building of resilience and insight within the young person. This will result in the parent/carers gaining new personal skills and knowledge that will serve as a protection against future self-harm. So the context of the young person who has self-harmed is very important. We know that young people find it difficult at times of stress to communicate their feelings directly. There are a number of reasons for this – some obvious, others not so.

The obvious reasons are usually to do with some degree of shame or self-blame. Telling a parent or close relative something painful and sensitive can feel like too much for some young people who prefer to talk to a friend, or in confidence to someone else such as a school counsellor, doctor or other professional. There are also many internet helplines or websites which are easily accessible to young people as a resource to help and support them through difficult times in their lives. These websites (some of which are included at the end of this book) offer a mixture of neutral information about emotional or psychological problems, and chatroom forums where they can share details about themselves with a group of peers, and benefit from group support.

Or young people can access help and support via written information in a range of media including books, magazines and newspapers. Each of these sources can offer access to support, guidance and advice, which is different from that offered by parents who may have their own particular way of responding and which may be experienced by the young person as unhelpful. Neutral and confidential support therefore doesn't come loaded with parental factors, relationship dynamics and characteristics which can militate against using, or even understanding, the support being offered.

But another reason for young people finding it difficult to talk directly to a parent is when the young person perceives a lack of ability in their parent to cope with the information being conveyed. This perception may be inaccurate or based on previous experiences which are irrelevant to the current situation. The young person may see their parent as a vulnerable and needy person who is struggling to cope with life in general, and their parenting responsibilities in particular.

The parent may well have their own mental health problems which are openly acknowledged, or disguised by self-medication or drug and alcohol misuse. Either way the young person will seek to protect their parent from the extra burden of trying to cope with a child, who has significant emotional problems, by hiding their own problem and even denying they have any problems if asked.

Problems can quickly escalate in situations where parent and young person are seeking to be open and honest, yet at the same time trying to protect themselves from disagreement, conflict or argument, while not wishing to add extra stress to the other person. If matters spiral out of control (and they can do so rapidly) then at some point the problems will become public and come to the attention of school, college and other welfare agencies.

Although these times can feel like crises and increase distress, in the long term they can be beneficial in triggering responses from outside professionals who can intervene, negotiate and support both parent and young person. Skilled support can not only deal with the immediate problems but also the underlying issues that may have been developing over quite some time, and lead to an improvement in relationships and the mental health issues of all involved.

How can friends and family help?

If a parent/carer discovers that someone they love and care about is self-harming, it can be very difficult to cope with their own feelings of shock, anger, guilt, grief and helplessness. They may be very afraid of what might happen.

Professional staff should try to enlist the help of family, friends and other appropriate professionals to support them. Although they may feel helpless, what you as a professional worker do or don't do can make a lot of difference. If you encourage the parent/carer to pay due attention to the young person's injuries, they are affirming that they and their body are worth caring about. But parent/carers don't need to focus only on the injuries. It's important that they appreciate how difficult their child or relative is finding life. Professionals need to encourage the parent/carer to understand it will matter a great deal by showing the young person they want to understand.

They can begin by gently encouraging them to examine their feelings and to talk to someone about why they self-harm. They may find what their child or relative has to say is very difficult to hear. If it feels too much for them, help them to find someone else to talk to the young person. It's possible for the parent/carer to be honest with them about their own feelings and not to panic, blame them, treat them as if they are mad, or make them feel guilty.

Being uncritical will help the young person feel accepted and cared for, instead of even more self-hating. They need to be encouraged to keep emphasising all the non-harming aspects of the young person's life to help develop and support their sense of self-worth.

Don't let parents/carers expect change to happen quickly; and don't hold on to any expectation that their friend or relative can stop self-harming just because they want them to. People who self-harm are trying to resist feeling the full weight of their emotions. This defence mechanism can't be dismantled easily. It takes time for people to learn that their feelings won't destroy them. It's important parents/carers resist the temptation to step in constantly, to try to solve the problem. In the end, each individual young person has to draw on their own strengths and find their own healing inner resources.

Typical parent/carer thoughts and feelings are: fear, distress, confusion, worry, anger, anxiety and self-blame.

Their first reactions may be to remove the things that they are using to harm themselves, to be forceful in seeking help (e.g. urgently seeing a GP), to apply pressure on them to talk, or be confrontational. Self-harm is primarily a coping strategy. Until the reasons behind the self-harm have been explored taking away their ability to cope can be very detrimental.

The link to suicide

A common fear is that a loved one is feeling suicidal. Whilst some individuals that self-harm may have suicidal feelings, these are likely to originate from the issues behind the self-harm rather than the self-harm itself (Rowan 2001). Self-harm, as a coping mechanism, is very often a way of avoiding suicide by releasing thoughts, feelings and emotions. This is an important and counter-intuitive idea to get across to parents/carers. The reasons behind self-harm will need to be addressed when the individual is ready and with the right care and support. Appropriate specialist professional help may be needed. Whilst these reasons are being worked through the greatest support the parent/carer can offer is a listening ear. Less is more – in other words doing something needs to be replaced by *being something*.

Distractions can be a powerful way of diverting feelings of self-harm, or finding other ways to express thoughts and feelings such as poetry, art, sport, etc. Alternatives to self-harm such as ice cubes on the skin, flicking elastic bands or drawing on the skin with a red pen can also help. The table below gives more detailed dos and don'ts.

Children and young people suffering mental health problems who self-harm usually do so in the context of a family, or similar situation – there are usually other people nearby in close contact. The idea of supporting children indirectly by supporting parents/carers and other family members is not new but is gaining in social policy and therapeutic service responses. Family support is increasingly becoming a focus for intensive child and adolescent mental health preventive or treatment work (Walker 2006).

TABLE 4.1 DOS AND DON'TS WITH
SELF-HARMING YOUNG PEOPLE

Things to do	Things not to do
Open up methods of communication	Don't force them to talk about it
Give them the option to come to talk to you IF they want to	Don't make them feel that this is something that should be kept secret and is wrong to talk about, or that they have to talk about it
Ask them if they want to talk about what, if anything led to the individual episode of self-harm	Don't assume every episode of self-harm is for the same reason

Social context

The emotional well-being of children and young people in the UK falls behind those in Estonia, Greece and Slovenia. The UK was recently ranked 23 out of 43 'more developed' countries for children's well-being (Save the Children 2011).

The upward trend in child and adolescent mental health problems and specific increases in self-harm provide examples of situations where issues about the focus of intervention and the form of intervention require serious attention (CAMHS Review 2008). Are these manifestations of something inherently wrong with the modern family, or are they the social consequences of the impact of centralised state-controlled economies or unfettered, rapacious free market economic expansion? In other words should professional staff be trying to help parents cope better with the emotional and behavioural needs of a new generation of children and young people, or help families and communities challenge the prevailing socio-economic structures that produce such negative effects? Or should they be trying to do both at the same time?

Unencumbered market economics and regimes have had a significant impact on social policy in the industrialised world and have contributed substantially to redrawing the role of the state, particularly with regards to the provision of welfare resources.

The catastrophic world economic collapse in 2010 was the latest manifestation of the fragility of the economic context and the implications for social and welfare systems to cope with the consequences. As the limitations of capitalist laissez faire economics are revealed by unemployment and massive differences in wealth between countries, so global opposition to the social, environmental and psychological consequences increases (Harvey 2011).

Equally, in oppressive state-controlled command economies where human rights are restricted and personal freedoms seriously curtailed, the economic and social system of government will affect how citizens feel about themselves and their children in terms of self-esteem and emotional well-being. There is no perfect model because whichever social and economic context families live within, there are some who will thrive and others who will suffer depending on their own very personal strengths, weaknesses, coping abilities and genetic pre-dispositions.

We can assist in supporting and mobilising people who seek to liberate and empower themselves and orient their activities in providing assistance for one another and meeting their collective welfare needs. Working with children and families where mental health and emotional well-being are at risk offers the opportunity to make a difference to how people feel about themselves and the society of which they are part.

With marginalised and disenfranchised families this can be an important path towards re-connecting with their community, neighbours and other support systems. Feeling valued and cared for can be part of the social regeneration of a neighbourhood as important as its economic regeneration with desirable impacts on children's mental health and reduced levels of self-harm and suicide (Ferguson and Lavalette 2004).

Equally, the widening gap between rich and poor highlight the needs of those families socially excluded, marginalised and disempowered, causing strong feelings of resentment, envy and anger. Increased numbers of mothers in work, the ageing of the population, rise in youth homelessness, increased reporting of domestic violence, child abuse, and the prevalence of substance misuse, are cited as evidence of the financial pressures and relationship strains put on modern family life (Rowan 2001).

The social policy debate divides between those who blame lax child-rearing practices and the permissive 1960s, and those who cite the growth of individualism and the failures of capitalist economics to fulfil society's welfare needs.

Community developments

Racism and xenophobia have increased as European Union enlargement has accelerated migration, and armed conflict has precipitated increased numbers of asylum seekers. These are crucially important issues in other developed nations where immigration pressures are testing the capacity of social and welfare systems to manage their needs. The consequent economic and social dislocation has prompted more refugee applications or illegal immigration to wealthier countries (Sveaass and Reichelt 2001).

Already impoverished communities in the USA, Australia, Canada and the UK have been incited to regard families fleeing persecution, ethnic cleansing and political oppression as an unwelcome burden and part of their economic problems. These changes in the socio-geographic texture are mirrored in other countries producing similar moral panics and hasty policy changes to tackle the consequences.

At the latest census over 3 million (5.5%) of the 59 million people in Britain did not classify themselves as white. Half are South Asian (that is of Indian, Pakistani, and Bangladeshi descent) and 30 per cent are black. The rich diversity of Britain's minority populations reveals that nearly half of Britain's non-white population had been born in Britain, with three-quarters of these registered British citizens.

The overwhelming majority of non-white children under 16 were therefore born in Britain. Issues of citizenship and nationality, race and immigration provide the overarching context within legislation and public policy which sets the scene for racist and oppressive practice to go unchecked, increasing the self-hatred and low self-esteem that trigger self-harm.

How can young people help themselves?

If you are working with a young person who has already or is thinking about self-harming, or if they know someone close to them who is self-harming, it is worth considering the following. They can be re-assured that the feelings of self-harm will go away after a while. If they can cope with their upset without self-harming for a time, it will get easier over the next few hours. You can advise the young person as follows.

Advice for when they want to harm themselves

- Talk to someone – if they are on their own perhaps they could phone a friend. Telephone helplines and helpful contacts are listed at the end of this book.

- If the person they are with is making them feel worse, go out.

- Distract themselves by going out, listening to music, or by doing something harmless that interests them.

- Relax and focus their mind on something pleasant – their very own personal comforting place.

- Find another way to express their feelings such as squeezing ice cubes (which they can make with red juice to mimic blood if the sight of blood is important), or just drawing red lines on their skin.

- Give themselves some 'harmless pain' – eat a hot chilli, or have a cold shower.

- Focus their mind on positive things.

- Be kind to themselves – allowing them to do something harmless that they enjoy.

- Write a diary or a letter, to explain what is happening to them – no one else needs to see it.

Advice for when they don't feel like harming themselves

When the urge has gone, and they feel safe, suggest they think about the times that they have self-harmed and what (if anything) has been helpful such as:

- Go back in their mind to the last time when they did not want to self-harm, and move forward in their memory from there.

- Think about where they were, who they were with, and what they were feeling.

- Try to help them work out why they began feeling like they did.

- Did their self-harm give them a sense of escape, or relief, or control? Try to work out something to do that might give them the same result, but that doesn't cause damage.

- How did other people react?

- Could they have done anything else?

- Make a tape or MP3 recording. Talk about their good points and why they don't want to self-harm. Or ask someone they trust to do this. When they start to feel bad, they can play this back to remind them of the parts that are good and worthwhile.

- Make a 'crisis plan' so they can talk to someone instead of self-harming. Being able to get in touch with someone quickly can help them control their urge to self-harm. While they are talking, they may discover their wish to harm starts to go away.

What if they don't want to stop self-harming?

If they decide that they don't want to stop self-harming, they can still:

- reduce the damage to their body (e.g. by using clean blades if they cut themselves)

- keep thinking about possible answers to the things that make them harm themselves

- every so often, re-consider their decision not to stop.

What can a young person do if they know someone who self-harms?

It can be very upsetting to be close to someone who self-harms – but there are things they can do. The most important is to listen to them without judging them or being critical. This can be very hard if you are upset – and perhaps angry – about what they are doing. Try to encourage this young person to concentrate on their friend rather than their own feelings – although this can be hard.

Do:

- encourage them to talk to their friend when they feel like self-harming. Try to understand their feelings, and then move the conversation on to other things

- take some of the mystery out of self-harm by helping their friend find out about self-harm perhaps by showing them useful leaflets, or by using the internet or the local library

- find out about getting help – maybe suggest they go with their friend to see someone, such as their GP

- help their friend to think about their self-harm not as a shameful secret, but as a problem to be sorted out.

Don't:

- try to be their therapist (unless, of course, you are!). Therapy is complicated and they have enough to deal with as their friend, partner or relative

- expect their friend to stop overnight – it's difficult and takes time and effort

- react strongly, with anger, hurt, or upset – this is likely to make their friend feel worse. Talk honestly about the effect it has on them, but do this calmly and in a way that shows how much they care for them

- struggle with them when they are about to self-harm – it's better to walk away and to suggest they come and talk about it rather than do it

- make their friend promise not to do it again or make their involvement with them the basis for an agreement for stopping

- make themselves responsible for their friend's self-harm or become the person who is supposed to stop them. They must get on with their own life as well. Make sure they also talk to someone close, so they get some support.

The journey to recovery

It is important that plans developed from any assessment set clear goals, the first of which should be to avoid accidental death. The worker or parent/carer might usefully generate suggestions on what decisions might help end the self-harming behaviour.

One example might be to ensure they spend a lot of time in public places so they do not isolate themselves. This might counter the risk of self-harm in privacy since this is usually the location for such an act. Other tasks might include having the young person examine the short-term advantages of self-harm with the long-term consequences (such as scars or accidental death).

Another important goal is to try to reduce environmental stress by slowly but surely increasing the young person's connection to parents, friends and peer groups to improve communication skills, develop effective measures of self-soothing that do not include self-harm, and improve mood and emotional regulation. As such, the identification of stressors within the home and school is an important part of the work, as is the plan to decrease such stressors. There are many useful ways to engage the young person in finding alternative coping mechanisms. Parents can do much to encourage and reinforce these which may include:

- avoiding spending long periods on their own

- doing something creative such as painting

- doing calming activities or relaxation exercises

- making time for activities that they enjoy

- phoning a supportive friend for a chat.

It may take the young person a long time before they are ready to give up self-harm completely. They may even find that their need for it increases as they explore distressing experiences in their past that may underlie their self-harm, or make changes in the way that they live their life. Try not to let them get discouraged. The more progress they can make in sorting out other areas of their life, the easier giving up self-harm will eventually become.

Although many parents/carers consider it irrational, it is important that professionals do not aggressively discourage the young person from engaging in acts of self-harm. Rules place restrictions on their freedom.

When we maintain the right to choose, our choices are much more powerful and effective. Telling a young person not to injure her/himself is both aversive and condescending. Because self-harm is used as a method of coping and is often used as an attempt to relieve emotional distress when other methods have failed, it is essential for the person to have this option. Most young people would choose to not hurt themselves if they could.

Although self-harm produces feelings of shame, secrecy, guilt and isolation, it continues to be utilised as a method of coping. That young people will engage in self-harming behaviours despite the many negative effects is a clear indication of the necessity of this action to their survival. It is really important that support, and not limits, are offered to that young person. Self-harm should be viewed as a way of coping.

Whilst self-harm appears dangerous and destructive, it actually may be an attempt at self-healing or self-preservation. Many young people who self-harm are victims and are finding a coping mechanism for themselves.

The impact of supporting young people who self-harm

Research tells us that medical staff in particular find it difficult to manage, treat and support young people who self-harm. The initial feelings aroused probably include shock, fear, disgust and anger towards the young person (Kent and Read 1998).

How can a person deliberately inflict harm on themselves or mutilate their bodies? This confounds staff who have been trained to help people – usually the victims of a disease, accident, or genetic disorder beyond their control.

The difficulty in this work, and for parents trying to understand and help, is that the young person is usually in a very unco-operative mood, extremely distressed, untalkative and hostile to intrusive questioning. Tension and arguments can escalate, with accusation and counter-accusations creating a blaming culture. This pattern of relationship established between the young person and those trying to help can quickly deteriorate and make matters worse.

Medical staff can easily feel that they have more important patients to attend to and begin to display indifference and an uncaring attitude. Research confirms these attitudes are quite prevalent on hospital wards where the young person will initially be placed (Timimi and Maitra 2005).

So it is essential that staff and parents obtain a lot of support to understand, process and make sense of their own feelings to make sure they find positive ways to cope, be helpful and emotionally available to the young person.

In essence staff and parents need to focus on communication and relationship-building skills and to nurture self-confidence, self-esteem and feelings of hope in the young person. Enlightened and progressive voluntary, public and self-help groups can do much valuable work to encourage parents to meet with others in similar situations to offer mutual support and encouragement.

For staff who work directly with young people who self-harm it is essential that they receive regular supervision separate from line management workload planning or administrative matters. The more the professional is able to recognise and manage their own feelings about the work and specific young people, the better able they will be to help.

Young people already suspicious, feeling guilty and resentful will quickly sense if a nurse, social worker or counsellor is nervous, unsure or anxious and this will result in the young person feeling mistrustful or unconfident in the adult. Specialist groups of staff in the same profession or facility can undertake very helpful group supervision, or individuals can seek out someone with deep experience of self-harm and supporting staff in individual supervision or consultation.

Reflective practice in a safe non-judgemental context will enhance a staff member's confidence and improve their skills and knowledge-building (Higham 2009).

Confidentiality

The duties of protecting young people from harming themselves and the ethical principles of client confidentiality are very important and tricky issues. Confidentiality by protecting clients from unauthorised disclosure of personal information during a professional therapeutic or counselling relationship is a well-established expectation.

This means that a young person receiving crucial help can do so with the secure trust necessary for them to make full disclosures about the circumstances and background to their self-harming behaviour without fear of exposure.

The duty to protect young people from harming themselves is an especially important professional responsibility, but this conflicts with the aim of confidentiality intended to assure the right to privacy, and a therapist is ethically obliged to refrain from revealing private client information – unless given authorisation to do so.

There are exceptions when confidentiality can be broken and these should be explained to the young person before any therapeutic help commences:

- when a therapist is involved in legal action arising from the therapy

- when a waiver to confidentiality has been previously obtained

- when the young person discloses child abuse, incest or neglect which must then be reported to other professionals.

The most difficult situation can arise when the young person talks about the prospects of self-harm and the therapist has to consider their legal/professional/employee duty to report any risk of harm to a vulnerable young person. Risk assessment is notoriously difficult and research consistently demonstrates that whatever model of risk assessment is used, it is flawed and not useful in predictive capacity as we noted earlier.

The dilemma for the person trying to help a young person suffering is to try to determine the level and immediacy of the self-harm and balancing the risk to the trust required for sensitive therapy to continue uninterrupted. If a young person cannot feel safe enough to express possibly disturbing thoughts and feelings then the foundation of therapy crumbles.

A salutary point to note is that failure to prevent suicide has become a leading reason for successful malpractice legal claims against therapists.

Young people's voices

Research (Timimi and Maitra 2005) shows that when young people are consulted about the kind of support they actually find helpful the key factors are:

- confidentiality

- having choice

- feeling respected.

Crucial factors in the research is that young people feel strongly about the degree of control they are allowed, both towards their self-harm and the meaning this has for them. Trying to control young people only makes matters worse.

Counselling as a form of support is viewed positively but this raised the issue of confidentiality discussed earlier. Also having a counselling service available in schools is problematic because it soon becomes clear to other school students who is seeing the counsellor and why. The stigma and shame associated with self-harm should never be underestimated, nor the cruel way some young people use another's vulnerability to exploit and bully.

A good, helpful and accessible service should include the following:

- removal of access to means of self-harm such as medication

- respect

- acknowledging stigma and shame

- working with feelings of hopelessness and impulsivity

- alternative coping strategies
- a collaborative rather than controlling relationship.

Future prospects

There is little research available to make useful predictions about the future prospects for young people who self-harm. The numbers of people who are at increased risk of further self-harm or suicide is small, as is the prospects for later adult personality disturbance, poor relationship skills and low social skills. However, the data on these issues is relatively small and methodologically variable in quality (Fox and Hawton 2004).

Young people often do not attend follow-up support and treatment, or they are unwilling to comply with long-term research. Support services need to constantly investigate and research to ensure they are accessible and efficacious. Each new generation of adolescents will require help that is tailored to their specific needs, experiences and perceptions, rather than being expected to fit into existing out of date provision. For example, intranet resources led by children themselves of children's charities are becoming more common and designed in a modern, appealing way to a generation used to accessing visual imagery and information on-line.

The long-term consequences

Cutting

It's important to remember that all injuries will leave permanent scarring. This can come as a surprise to people who expect to have their scars removed, when often there's very little that can be done.

As well as scarring, cutting skin can have more serious consequences. If the young person is cutting their wrist, they are risking long-term damage to the whole arm. Lots of young people who have injured nerves, or blood vessels can have them repaired, but if they cut a major nerve in a wrist they can be left with permanent weakness or numbness in their hand, or both.

There are steps the young person can be advised to take if they are going to cut that can help reduce the long-term effects. The first is to avoid doing it deeply. Second, it's important to get help so that wounds won't become infected, as that always makes scarring worse. Finally, try to persuade them against making cuts all over their body; cuts limited to a small area will mean smaller wounds and less scarring.

Burning

Burning is similar to cutting in that it causes damage to the skin and can leave a scar. Burning with a cigarette will leave a small – rather painful – scar, but not really any long-term consequences; however using chemicals or acids can cause massive destruction and people can even lose limbs. Potentially it can be life-threatening.

Head-banging

Because of the fragility of the head and brain, repeatedly banging the head against a wall or another object could do long-term damage. While there hasn't been particular research into head-banging as a form of self-harm, researchers have investigated whether footballers are at risk of brain damage through heading footballs. Jeff Astle died in 2002 from a brain disease caused by constantly heading footballs.

Overdosing

The effects of drug overdose will vary depending on what was taken, and the quantity. The main organs affected by paracetamol overdoses are the liver and kidneys. Assuming the initial effects are treated, there is still a chance that long-term organ damage can occur. The main thing to do is get checked out as soon as possible following an overdose – usually in Casualty or A&E.

For long-term follow-up and advice, the GP, or possibly a CAMHS specialist, should be involved to help the young person.

Conclusion

If you're worried that a young person's self-harming may lead to some of these longer-term effects, now might be a good time to try and help them take some initial steps towards recovery.

This can seem like a daunting prospect, but if you take it one stage at a time it may feel more achievable. As we have noted earlier, one of the most effective ways to help and support them take their first steps is to use coping tips and distractions to deal with self-harming or suicidal urges. If they haven't done so already, confiding in someone they know, or even someone they don't, such as a doctor (GP) or professional counsellor, can also help you and them to reflect on things more objectively.

Young people tend to avoid formal procedures and systems located in schools, clinics or bureaucratic offices. Local projects with volunteers and peers who they can relate to are more successful in engaging them. Find out where, what and who they perceive as helpful rather than try to direct them only to what you know.

Knowing that person is there to support them through a difficult time can be a real comfort. It's a simple concept but often it's the smallest, insignificant thing a professional does, often unknowingly, that can have the biggest impact on a young person suffering unbearable feelings and self-destructive thoughts. Being there for them is often enough – at least to start with.

No Health Without Mental Health – A Cross Governmental Outcomes Strategy for People of All Ages*

There are two powerful themes to the new coalition government approach. First, the Government must demonstrate its commitment and do the things that only the Government can do – but it cannot, on its own, deliver the ambitions in this strategy. We are drawing on commitments across Whitehall departments, employers, schools, local authorities and the voluntary and community sector. We all have a part to play to meet the social and economic challenge posed by mental ill health, and to improve the well-being of the population.

Second, power is moving away from the centre. The concept of the Big Society captures this shift, whereby citizens take more control over their lives and build more capable communities. It is particularly relevant to mental health. We want more decisions about mental health taken locally, with more flexibility for local people to make decisions based on local needs.

Our approach is based on the principles that the Government has laid down for its health reforms:

- Putting people who use services at the heart of everything we do – 'No decision about me without me' is the governing principle. Care should be personalised to reflect people's needs, not those of the professional or the system. People should have access

---

* London: Department of Health (2011). Crown copyright, with permission.

to the information and support they need to exercise
choice of provider and treatment.

- Focusing on measurable outcomes and the NICE
  Quality Standards that deliver them rather than top–
  down process targets.

- Empowering local organisations and practitioners
  to have the freedom to innovate and to drive
  improvements in services that deliver support of
  the highest quality for people of all ages, and all
  backgrounds and cultures.

The Government is investing around £400 million over the
next four years to make a choice of psychological therapies
available for those who need them in all parts of England, and
is expanding provision for children and young people, older
people, people with long-term physical health problems and
those with severe mental illness.

We know the conditions that foster well-being. We know
many of the factors that help people to recover from mental
health problems and live the lives they want to lead. We
know the interconnections between mental health, housing,
employment and safe communities. This strategy builds on
that knowledge, sets out the ambitions the Government
shares with its partners and against which it will be judged,
and invites others to join us in making better mental health
for all a reality.

Executive summary

1.1 Mental health is everyone's business – individuals, families,
employers, educators and communities all need to play their
part. Good mental health and resilience are fundamental to
our physical health, our relationships, our education, our
training, our work and to achieving our potential. The Prime
Minister and the Deputy Prime Minister have made it clear

that success for the Coalition Government will be assessed not just on bringing about a healthy economy but also on the well-being of the whole population. Moreover, good mental health and well-being also bring wider social and economic benefits. But to realise these benefits, we all need to take action and be supported by the Government to do so. We all need to take responsibility for caring for our own mental health and that of others, and to challenge the blight of stigma and discrimination. Our objectives for employment, for education, for training, for safety and crime reduction, for reducing drug and alcohol dependence and homelessness cannot be achieved without improvements in mental health.

1.2 This mental health outcomes strategy looks to communities, as well as the state, to promote independence and choice, reflecting the recent vision for adult social care. It sets out how the Government, working with all sectors of the community and taking a life course approach, will:

- improve the mental health and well-being of the population and keep people well; and

- improve outcomes for people with mental health problems through high-quality services that are equally accessible to all.

1.3 This is a strategy for people of all ages, and throughout this document we will use the word 'people' to encompass infants, children, young people, working-age adults and older people.

1.4 While this strategy is specific to England, the challenges are common across the four countries of the UK. We will work closely with the Devolved Administrations in Northern Ireland, Scotland and Wales, recognising their particular and varying responsibilities. Each will consider the most appropriate arrangements to address the issues in ways that meet their own circumstances and needs.

Mental health is everyone's business – a call to action

1.5 A wide range of partner organisations, including user and carer representatives, providers, local government and government departments, have worked with the Department of Health to agree a set of shared objectives to improve mental health outcomes for individuals and the population as a whole. The six shared objectives are as follows:

1. More people will have good mental health. More people of all ages and backgrounds will have better well-being and good mental health. Fewer people will develop mental health problems – by starting well, developing well, working well, living well and ageing well.

2. More people with mental health problems will recover. More people who develop mental health problems will have a good quality of life – greater ability to manage their own lives, stronger social relationships, a greater sense of purpose, the skills they need for living and working, improved chances in education, better employment rates and a suitable and stable place to live.

3. More people with mental health problems will have good physical health. Fewer people with mental health problems will die prematurely, and more people with physical ill health will have better mental health.

4. More people will have a positive experience of care and support. Care and support, wherever it takes place, should offer access to timely, evidence-based interventions and approaches that give people the greatest choice and control over their own lives, in the least restrictive environment, and should ensure that people's human rights are protected.

5. Fewer people will suffer avoidable harm. People receiving care and support should have confidence that the services they use are of the highest quality and at least as safe as any other public service.

6. Fewer people will experience stigma and discrimination. Public understanding of mental health will improve and, as a result, negative attitudes and behaviours to people with mental health problems will decrease. Why do we need a new outcomes strategy for mental health?

1.6 If we are to build a healthier, more productive and fairer society in which we recognise difference, we have to build resilience, promote mental health and well-being, and challenge health inequalities. We need to prevent mental ill health, intervene early when it occurs, and improve the quality of life of people with mental health problems and their families.

1.7 Improved mental health and well-being is associated with a range of better outcomes for people of all ages and backgrounds. These include improved physical health and life expectancy, better educational achievement, increased skills, reduced health risk behaviours such as smoking and alcohol misuse, reduced risk of mental health problems and suicide, improved employment rates and productivity, reduced anti-social behaviour and criminality, and higher levels of social interaction and participation. These issues will be further explored in a suite of public mental health evidence reviews to be published shortly by the Department of Health.

1.8 Some mental health problems** are long lasting and can significantly affect the quality of people's lives, especially if they are not treated. Some people only experience a single episode of mental ill health. Others, who may have longer-standing problems, can enjoy a high quality of life and fulfilling careers. However, the personal, social and economic costs of mental ill health can be considerable. No other health area combines frequency of occurrence with persistence and breadth of impact to the same extent. The stigma attached to mental ill health and the social barriers that surround it amplify its direct effects and damage the life chances of people with mental health problems.

1.9 There are indications that some problems are becoming more prevalent: for example, more young people have behavioural and emotional problems. The incidence of mental health problems – including in young people – can increase in times of economic and employment uncertainty, as can the rate of suicide. The number of older people in our population is growing, with a corresponding increase in the number of those at risk of dementia and depression.

**   Note on terms used in this strategy: The phrase 'mental health problem' is used in this strategy as an umbrella term to describe the full range of diagnosable mental illnesses and disorders, including personality disorder. Mental health problems may be more or less common, may be acute or longer lasting and may vary in severity. They manifest themselves in different ways at different ages and may (e.g. in children and young people) present as behavioural problems. Some people object to the use of terms such as 'mental health problems' on the grounds that they medicalise ways of thinking and feeling and do not acknowledge the many factors that can prevent people from reaching their potential. We recognise these concerns and the stigma attached to mental ill health; however, there is no universally acceptable terminology that we can use as an alternative.

Mental health problems – the statistics

- At least one in four people will experience a mental health problem at some point in their life and one in six adults has a mental health problem at any one time.

- One in ten children aged between 5 and 16 years has a mental health problem, and many continue to have mental health problems into adulthood.

- Half of those with lifetime mental health problems first experience symptoms by the age of 14, and three-quarters before their mid-20s.

- Self-harming in young people is not uncommon (10–13% of 15–16-year-olds have self-harmed).

- Almost half of all adults will experience at least one episode of depression during their lifetime.

- One in ten new mothers experiences postnatal depression.

- About 1 in 100 people has a severe mental health problem.

- Some 60 per cent of adults living in hostels have a personality disorder.

- Some 90 per cent of all prisoners are estimated to have a diagnosable mental health problem (including personality disorder) and/or a substance misuse problem.

The Short-Term Physical and Psychological Management and Secondary Prevention of Self-Harm in Primary and Secondary Care*

Staff attitudes and young people's experiences

There is a rich and well-established service user literature on the subject of self-harm, particularly regarding the acts and meanings of self-harm from the service users' point of view (Harrison, Moller and Bordeaux 2011). From this emerges a picture of self-harm as an activity that is usually done in private, and which forms part of an individual's coping mechanisms. However, when the acts are made public, misunderstandings and lack of awareness in clinical practice, both in general medicine and psychiatry, can lead to service responses that are not only unhelpful, but may make matters worse for people who self-harm. This lack of understanding, and the fear thus engendered, can manifest itself in the attitudes, language and treatment of service users who self-harm.

Carers may relieve their disappointment and frustration with the patient by stigmatising her as bad, attention seeking or manipulative, terms which have no explanatory value but do subtly devalue the patient's distress and can sometimes be used to justify either harsh or indifferent treatment. It is

---

*   National Clinical Practice Guideline Number 16: National Collaborating Centre for Mental Health commissioned by the National Institute for Clinical Excellence (2004). Crown copyright, with permission.

also arguable that apparently therapeutic manoeuvres such as ECT, high-dose medication, or the transfer of care may on occasions be a means of getting rid of a frustrating patient or even punishing her for her refractoriness (Tantam and Whittaker 1992).

Health services aim to minimise harm and therefore try as a priority to reduce or prevent self-harm. Many healthcare professionals view self-harm as attempted suicide, and few healthcare professionals consider or discuss the meaning, function or intention of acts of self-harm, instead assuming that suicide was intended and should be prevented as far as possible. But in attempting to prevent a person from hurting him- or herself, rather than looking at the underlying causes of such behaviour, or indeed the function such behaviour serves a particular individual, services can inadvertently either exacerbate the behaviour or 'drive it underground'. Good practice guidelines developed by users recommend that stopping self-harm should not be a goal of treatment, nor should treatment or care be withheld as a condition of stopping self-harm (Bird and Faulkner 2000).

Unfortunately, many people who self-harm, especially those who do so repeatedly, feel that healthcare professionals are not willing to listen to them and are not interested in reading the wealth of literature regarding self-harm written by service users. This literature not only relates the experience of self-harm and its treatment from the perspective of service users, it also suggests new practices that would address the problems faced by them.

Service users often regard themselves as experts by experience, but feel that many healthcare professionals disregard service user literature as somehow lacking authority, a situation that is no longer sustainable in the light of recent policy developments. For example, the Department of Health's expert patient programme (DoH 2001) acknowledges that in some conditions the patient may understand the condition as well as, or better than, the clinician: 'this knowledge and experience held by the patient has for too long been an untapped resource. It is something that could greatly benefit the quality of patients' care and ultimately their quality of life, but which has been largely ignored in the past' (DoH 2006, p.97).

It is clear from both the existing literature and the focus groups that users consider the main cause of their poor experiences of services to be staff attitudes towards people who self-harm and the generally low level of staff understanding of self-harming behaviour. They do not treat people who self-harm seriously. This is supported by respondents in other studies:

> [The nurse was] 'pretty impatient with me'. (Anon 2000)

> Doesn't treat me like a normal [sic], as if I'm not normal because I self-harm, like there's something wrong with my intelligence or something. Like a retard, I suppose. Because I self-harm, then obviously I'm thick. (Respondent about his GP; Bywaters and McCleod 2003)

> Got no help at all. All they wanted to do is pick on me like I was a naughty little girl, and it made me angry, and I couldn't open up at all for how they treated me. I just dreaded going to see them. (Harris 2000)

> She said, 'you are trying to disgust me'.

> … He doesn't understand and like uses horrible words like 'mutilation'.

Not only do these kinds of attitudes make users' experiences of services unpleasant, but they can also increase service users' levels of distress. Indeed some service users felt these attitudes lead to further self-harm and to people treating their own wounds to avoid attending an emergency department (e.g. Harris 2000). Focus group respondents reported increased distress as a result of the interactions they have had with staff. In particular, they report feelings of isolation and humiliation that encourage them to self-harm again as a way of coping with the distress and to avoid services in future:

> …it made me even more and more distressed and I've actually felt like leaving the hospital and going and self-harming again because that's the only way I can deal with the distress.

> …even if my life was in danger…I'd rather sit at home and sit it out and see whether I'd survived than risk the humiliation.

Useful Resources and Organisations

United Kingdom

Asian Family Counselling Services
74 The Avenue
London W13 8LB
Tel: 020 8997 5749

BBC Health Advice
www.bbc.co.uk/health/emotion_health

Black Information Link
The 1990 Trust
9 Cranmer Road
London SW9 6EJ
Tel: 020 7582 1990
www.blink.org.uk

Child Psychotherapy Trust
Star House
104–108 Grafton Road
London NW5 4BD
Tel: 020 7284 1355
www.cpt.co.uk

Childline
2nd Floor, Royal Mail Building
50 Studd Street
London N1 0QW
Tel: 020 7239 1000
www.childline.org.uk

Department of Health
Richmond House
79 Whitehall
London SW1A 2NS
www.dh.gov.uk

FOCUS
The Royal College of Psychiatrists
College Research Unit
6th Floor
83 Victoria Street
London SW1H 0HW
Tel: 020 7227 0821
www.rcpsych.ac.uk/cru

Harmless
PO Box 9325
Nottingham NG8 9FB
www.harmless.org.uk

NCH Action for Children
85 Highbury Park
London N5 1UD
Tel: 020 7704 7000
www.nchafc.org.uk

NSPCC
National Centre
42 Curtain Road
London EC2A 3NH
Tel: 020 7825 2500
www.nspcc.org.uk

National Association of Young People's
Counselling and Advisory Services
17–23 Albion Road
Leicester LE1 6GD
Tel: 01642 816846

National Centre for Eating Disorders
54 New Road
Esher
Surrey KT10 9NU
Tel: 01372 469493
www.eating-disorders.org.uk

National Self Harm Network
PO Box 7264
Nottingham NG1 6WJ
www.nshn.co.uk

Recoveryourlife.com
RYL
Magdalen House
3 Magdalen Street
Eye
Suffolk IP23 7AJ
www.recoveryourlife.com

Samaritans
The Upper Mill
Kingston Road
Ewell
Surrey KT17 2AF
www.samaritans.org.uk

Tavistock Institute
120 Belsize Lane
London NW3 5BA
Tel: 0207 435 7111
www.tav-port.org.uk

United Kingdom National Self-harm Network (NSHN)
PO Box 7264
Nottingham NG1 6WJ
Helpline: 0800 622 6000

Young Minds
48–50 St John Street
London EC1M 4DG
Tel: 020 7336 8445
www.youngminds.org.uk

Youth in Mind
www.youthinmind.net

YouthNet UK
The Site.Org
Stop self harming
www.thesite.org/heal

Canada

Association Canadienne Pour La Sante Mentale
Division du Québec
326–911 Jean-Talon Street Est
Montréal QC H2R 1V5
Tel: 514 849 3291
Fax: 514 849 8372
info@acsm.qc.ca
www.acsm.qc.ca

Canadian Mental Health Association

Alberta Division
320 Capital Place
9707–110 Street NW
Edmonton AB T5K 2L9
Tel: 780 482 6576
Fax: 780 482 6348
alberta@cmha.ab.ca
www.alberta.cmha.ca/

British Columbia Division
1200–1111 Melville Street
Vancouver BC V6E 3V6
Tel: 604 688 3234
Fax: 604 688 3236
info@cmha.bc.ca
www.cmha.bc.ca/

Manitoba Division
4 Fort Street
Suite 100
Winnipeg MB R3C 1C4
Tel: 204 953 2350
Fax: 204 775 3497
info@cmhamanitoba.ca
www.manitoba.cmha.ca

Newfoundland and Labrador Division
70 The Boulevard
1st Floor
St. John's NL A1A 1K2
Tel: 709 753 8550
Fax: 709 753 8537
office@cmhanl.ca
www.cmhanl.ca

Northwest Territories Division
5125 50th Street
PO Box 2580
Yellowknife, NT X1A 2P9
Tel: 867 873 3190
Fax: 867 873 4930
cmha@yk.com

Ontario Division
2301–180 Dundas St W.
Toronto ON M5G 1Z8
Tel: 416 977 5580
Fax: 416 977 2813
info@ontario.cmha.ca
www.ontario.cmha.ca

Saskatchewan Division
2702 12th Avenue
Regina SK S4T 1J2
Tel: 306 525 5601
Fax: 306 569 3788
contactus@cmhask.com
www.cmhask.com

Kids Help Telephone Canada
Tel: 1 800 668 6868
www.kidshelpphone.ca

Mental Health Canada
www.mentalhealthcanada.com

Prairie Womens Health Centre
PWHCE Administrative Centre – Winnipeg
56 The Promenade
Winnipeg MB R3B 3H9
Tel: (204) 982 6630
Fax: (204) 982 6637
E-mail: pwhce@uwinnipeg.ca

Recovery Canada – The Wellness Network
2–558 Upper Gage Avenue
Suite 250
Hamilton ON
L8V 4J6
Tel: (905) 389 3178
Fax: (905) 383 3200

United States

American Self Harm Information Clearing House
521 Temple Place
Seattle WA 98122
Helpline: 206 604 8963

Beyond Blue
PO Box 6100
Hawthorn West 3122
Victoria
Suicide Helpline Victoria: 1300 651 251
Kids Help Line (free call): 1800 55 1800
www.beyondblue.org.au

Mental Health America
2000 N. Beauregard Street
6th Floor
Alexandria VA 22311
Tel: (703) 684 7722
Toll free: (800) 969 6642
Fax: (703) 684 5968

National Institute of Mental Health
National Institute of Mental Health (NIMH)
Science Writing, Press, and Dissemination Branch
6001 Executive Boulevard, Room 8184, MSC 9663
Bethesda MD 20892–9663
Tel: 301 443 4513 (local)
Toll-free: 1 866 615 6464
Email: nimhinfo@nih.gov

Self Mutilators Anonymous
www.selfmutilatorsanonymous.org

Australia

AIHW National Injury Surveillance Unit
Mark Oliphant Building
Laffer Drive
Bedford Park SA 5042
Australia
Tel: (61) (08) 8374 0970
Fax: (61) (08) 8374 0702

Headspace National Office Australia
47–51 Chetwynd Street
North Melbourne
Victoria 3051.
Tel: 03 9027 0100
www.headspace.org.au

Lifeline Australia
Tel: 13 11 14

Mental Health Association
Level 5, 80 William St
East Sydney NSW 2011
Tel: (02) 9339 6000
Fax: (02) 9339 6066
E-mail: mha@mentalhealth.asn.au

Mental Health Information and Referral Service
Tel: 1300 131 114

Reach Out.Com
crew@reachout.com.au

References

AIHW (2001) Child Protection Australia, 1999–2000. Canberra: Australian Institute of Health and Welfare.

Bagley, C. and Mallick, K. (2000) 'How adolescents perceive their emotional life, behaviour, and self-esteem in relation to family stressors: A six-culture study.' In N. Singh, J. Leung and A. Singh *International Perspectives on Child and Adolescent Mental Health*. Oxford: Elsevier.

Bandura, A. (1986) *Social Foundations of Thought and Action: A Social Cognitive Perspective*. New Jersey: Prentice Hall.

Bernard, S. (2009) *Developing Mental Health Services for Children and Adolescents with Learning Disabilities: A Toolkit for Clinicians*. London: Royal College of Psychiatrists.

Bird, L. and Faulkner, A. (2000) *Suicide and Self Harm*. London: Mental Health Foundation.

Briggs, S. (2002) *Working with Adolescents – A Contemporary Psychodynamic Approach*. Basingstoke: Palgrave Macmillan.

Bywaters, P. and McCleod, E. (2003) 'Social care's impact on emergency medicine: A model to test.' *Emergency Medicine Journal 20* 134–137.

Calder, M. (2007) *Understanding, Assessing and Engaging with Young People who Self-Harm*. Lyme Regis: Russell House Publishers.

CAMHS Review (2008) *Children and Young People in Mind – Final Report of the CAMHS Review*. London: HMSO.

Caplan, G. (1961) *Principles of Preventive Psychiatry*. London: Basic Books.

Cooper, P. (ed.) (1999) *Understanding and Supporting Children with Emotional and Behavioural Difficulties*. London: Jessica Kingsley Publishers.

Department of Health (2001) *Children Looked After in England: 2000/2001*. London: HMSO.

DfES (2003) *Every Child Matters*. London: Department for Education and Science.

DfES (2006) *Youth Matters: Next Steps*. Nottingham: Department for Education and Skills.

Doel, M. and Marsh, P. (1992) *Task-Centred Social Work*. Aldershot: Ashgate.

DoH (2003) *Guidelines for the Appointment of General Practitioners with Special Interests in the Delivery of Clinical Services, Child Protection*. London: Department of Health Publications.

DoH (2004) *The Children Act*. London: Department of Health, HMSO.

DOH (2006) *The National Evaluation of the Pilot Phase of the Expert Patients programme- Final Report.* London: HMSO.

DoH (2007) *Promoting Mental Health for Children held in Secure Settings.* London: HMSO.

DoH (2011) *No Health without Mental Health – A Cross Governmental Outcomes Strategy for People of All Ages.* London: Department of Health.

DoH/DCSF (2005) *Common Assessment Framework.* London: HMSO.

Elliot, V. (2007) 'Interventions and services for refugee and asylum-seeking children and families.' In V. Postanis (ed.) *Mental Health Interventions and Services for Vulnerable Children and Young People.* London: Jessica Kingsley Publishers.

Ferguson, H. and Lavalette, M. (2004) 'Beyond power discourse: Alienation and social work.' *British Journal of Social Work 33,* 1005–1024.

Fernando, S. (2002) *Mental Health Race and Culture.* Basingstoke: Palgrave.

Fox, C. and Hawton, K. (2004) *Deliberate Self-Harm in Adolescence.* London: Jessica Kingsley Publishers.

Freeman, J., Epston, D. and Lobovits, D. (1997) *Playful Approaches to Serious Problems: Narrative Therapy with Children and Their Families.* New York: Norton.

Gilbert, P. (2003) *The Value of Everything – Social Work and its Importance in the Field of Mental Health.* Lyme Regis: Russell House Publishers.

Gorell-Barnes, G. (1984) *Working With Families.* Basingstoke: Macmillan/BASW.

Gorell-Barnes, G. (1998) *Family Therapy in Changing Times.* Basingstoke: Macmillan.

Hadfield, J. (1975) *Childhood and Adolescence.* London: Penguin.

Harris, J.R. (2000) 'Socialization, personality development, and the child's environments.' *Developmental Psychology 36,* 699–710.

Harrison, J., Moller, J. and Bordeaux, S. (2011) *Youth Suicide and Self-Injury Australia (15).* Flinders University, Adelaide: Research Centre for Injury Studies.

Harvey, D. (2011) *The Enigma of Capital and the Crisis of Capitalism.* New York: Profile Books.

Hawton, K., Rodham, K., Evans, E. and Weatherall, R. (2002) 'Deliberate self-harm in adolescents: Self report survey in schools in England.' *British Medical Journal 325,* 1207.

Hellinckx, W., Colton, M. and Williams, M. (1997) *International Perspectives on Family Support.* Aldershot: Ashgate Publishing.

Henderson, P. and Thomas, D. (1987) *Skills in Neighbourhood Work.* London: Allen and Unwin.

Heslop, P. and Macaulay, F. (2009) *Hidden Pain? Self-Injury and People with Learning Disabilities.* Bristol: Norah Fry Research Institute and Bristol Crisis Service for Women.

Higham, P. (2009) *Post-Qualifying Social Work Practice.* London: Sage.

Hodes, M. (2000) 'Psychologically distressed refugee children in the United Kingdom.' *Child Psychology and Psychiatry Review 5*, 2, 57–67.

Home Office (2008) *Crime in England and Wales.* London: HMSO.

House of Commons (2011) *Parlimentary Answers.* Hansard. London: HMSO.

Hughes, P. (1999) *Dynamic Psychotherapy Explained.* London: Radcliffe.

Ingham, R. (2008) *Research on Sexual Health of Young People – Challenges and Constraints.* University of Southampton: Centre for Sexual Health Research, AYPH Conference Presentation.

Kent, H. and Read, J. (1998) 'Measuring consumer participation in mental health services: Are attitudes related to professional orientation?' *International Journal of Social Psychiatry 44*, 4, 295–310.

Kiddle, C. (1999) *Traveller Children: A Voice for Themselves.* London: Jessica Kingsley Publishers.

Kurtz, Z., Thornes, R. and Wolkind, S. (1995) *Services for the Mental Health of Children and Young People in England: Assessment of Needs and Unmet Need.* London: HMSO.

Laye-Gindhu, A. and Schonert-Reichl, K.A. (2005) 'Nonsuicidal self-harm among community adolescents: Understanding the "whats" and "whys" of self-harm.' *Journal of Youth and Adolescence 34*, 5, 447–457.

Lemos, G. and Crane, P. (2011) Racism in the National Health Service (Unpublished NHS commissioned research) *Guardian Newspaper,* June 2011.

MacFarlane, A. and McPherson, A. (1995) 'Primary healthcare and adolescence.' *British Medical Journal 311*, 825–826.

MacNeil, G., Dressler, W.W. and Kaufman, A.V. (2000) 'Ethnic differences in risk factors associated with substance use in adolescence.' In N.N. Singh, J.P. Leung and A.N. Singh *International Perspectives on Child and Adolescent Mental Health.* London: Elsevier.

Marfe, E. (2003) 'Assessing risk following deliberate self-harm'. *Paediatric Nursing 15*, 8, 32–34.

McDougall, T. (2006) *Child and Adolescent Mental Health Nursing.* London: Blackwell.

Meltzer, H., Gatward, R., Goodman, R. and Ford, T. (2000) *Mental Health of Children and Adolescents in Great Britain.* London: HMSO.

Mental Health Foundation (1999) *The Big Picture: A National Survey of Child Mental Health in Britain.* London: Mental Health Foundation.

Mental Health Foundation (2002) *The Mental Health Needs of Young Offenders.* London: Mental Health Foundation.

Mental Health Foundation (2006) *Truth Hurts: Report of the National Inquiry into Self Harm among Young People.* London: Mental Health Foundation.

Mind (2009) *Making Sense of Cognitive Behaviour Therapy.* London: Mind.

Minuchin, S. (1974) *Families and Family Therapy.* London: Tavistock.

Morrison, L. and L'Heureux, J. (2001) 'Suicide and gay/lesbian/bisexual youth: Implications for clinicians.' *Journal of Adolescence 24,* 39–49.

NICE (2004) *Self-Harm: Short-Term Treatment and Management.* London: National Institute for Health and Clinical Excellence.

NICE (2005) *Depression in Children and Young People.* London: National Institute for Health and Clinical Excellence.

O'Brian, N., Moules, T. and Walker, S. (2010) *The Impact of Cyber-Bullying on Young People's Mental Health.* Research Report. Anglia Ruskin University/ National Children's Bureau.

Okitikpi, T. and Aymer, C. (2008) *The Art of Social Work Practice.* Lyme Regis: Russell House Publishers.

Oldman, C. and Beresford, B. (1998) *Disabled Children and their Families.* York: Joseph Rowntree Foundation.

ONS (2007) *Child and Adolescent Mental Health Statistics.* London: Office for National Statistics, HMSO.

ONS (2008) *Three Years On: Survey of Development and Emotional Wellbeing of Children and Young People.* London: Office for National Statistics.

Palmer, G. (2010) *The Poverty Site.* www.poverty.org.uk/18/index accessed 26 September 2011.

Pollock, S. and Boland, M. (1990) 'Children and HIV infection.' *New Jersey Psychologist 40,* 3, 17–21.

Refugee Action (2006) *The Destitution Trap.* London: Refugee London.

Richardson, G., Partridge, I. and Barrett, J. (2010) *Child and Adolescent Mental Health Services – An Operational Handbook,* 2nd edn. London: Royal College of Psychiatrists.

Richardson, J. and Joughin, C. (2000) *The Mental Health Needs of Looked After Children.* London: Gaskell.

Rowan, A. (2001) 'Adolescent Substance Abuse and Suicide.' *Depression and Anxiety 14,* 186–191.

Rutter, M. (1999) 'Preventing anti-social behaviour in young people: The contribution of early intervention'. In R. Bayley (ed.) *Transforming Children's Lives: The Importance of Early Intervention.* London: Family Policy Studies Centre.

Saravanan, B., Jacob, K.S., Prince, M., Bhugra, D. and David, A.S. (2004) 'Culture and Insight Revisited'. *British Journal of Psychiatry 184*, 107–109.

Save the Children (2011) *State of the World's Mothers*. London: Save the Children.

Schoon, I., Wiggins, R.D., Bynner, J., Joshi, H. and Parsons, S. (2002) *The Accumulation of Risk in the Life Course from Birth to Young Adulthood*. Brighton: Trust for Study of Adolescence/ESCR.

Sicile-Kira, C. (2003) *Autism Spectrum Disorders: The Complete Guide*. London: Vermillion.

Slee, N., Garnefski, N., van der Leeden, R., Arensman, E. and Spinhoven, P. (2008) 'Cognitive–behavioural intervention for self-harm: Randomised controlled trial.' *British Journal of Psychiatry 192*, 202–211.

Social Exclusion Unit (2002) *Reducing Re-Offending by Ex-Offenders*. London: HMSO.

Sveaass, N. and Reichelt, S. (2001) Refugee families in therapy: From referrals to therapeutic conversations. *Journal of Family Therapy 23*, 2, 119–136.

Tantam, D. and Whittaker, J. (1992) 'Personality disorder and self wounding.' *British Journal of Psychiatry 161*, 451–464.

Timimi, S. and Maitra, B. (2005) *Critical Voices in Child and Adolescent Mental Health*. London: Free Association Books.

Truth Hurts (2006) *Report of the National Inquiry into Self-harm among Young People*. London: Mental Health Foundation.

Van Ijzendoorn, M.H. and Sagi, A. (1997) 'Cross-cultural patterns of attachment: Universal and Contextual Dimensions'. In J. Cassidy and P.R. Shaver (eds) *Handbook of Attachment Theory, Research and Clinical Applications*. New York: Guilford Press.

Vincent, J.P. and Jouriles, E.N. (2000) *Domestic Violence, Guidelines for Research-Informed Practice*. London: Jessica Kingsley Publishers.

Walker, S. (2003a) *Social Work and Child and Adolescent Mental Health*. Lyme Regis: Russell House Publishers.

Walker, S. (2003b) 'Family support and family therapy – same difference?' *International Journal of Social Welfare 12*, 4, 307–314.

Walker, S. (2005) *Culturally Competent Therapy – Working with Children and Young People*. Basingstoke: Palgrave.

Walker, S. (2006) 'The morphing of family therapy and family support – how British social policy and feminist practice are interacting.' *Journal of Feminist Family Therapy 17*, 3/4, 1–22.

Walker, S. (2010) *The Social Worker's Guide to Child and Adolescent Mental Health*. London: Jessica Kingsley Publishers.

Walker, S. and Akister, J. (2004) *Applying Family Therapy, A Guide for Caring Professionals in the Community*. Lyme Regis: Russell House Publishers.

Walker, S. and Becket, C. (2011) *Social Work Assessment and Intervention*, 2nd edn. Lyme Regis: Russell House Publishers.

Walker, S. and Thurston, C. (2006) *Safeguarding Children and Young People – A Guide to Integrated Practice*. Lyme Regis: Russell House Publishers.

Whitlock, J., Lader, J. and Conterio, K. (2007) 'The internet and self-injury: What psychotherapists should know.' *Journal of Clinical Psychology 63*, 11, 1135–1143.

WHO (2009) *World Health Day*. Geneva: World Health Organization.

WHO (2011) *Assessment for Self-Harm/Suicide in Persons with Priority Mental, Neurological and Substance Use Disorders*. Mental Health Gap Prevention Programme. Geneva: World Health Organization, Evidence Resource Centre.

Woodhead, M. (1998) 'Understanding child development in the context of children's rights.' In C. Cunninghame (ed.) *Realising Children's Rights*. London: Save the Children.

Young Minds (2001) *Briefing on the NSF for Mental Health*. London: Young Minds.

Index